France

ENGLISH CHANNEL

ENGLAND

BAY OF BISCAY

BELGIUM

GERMANY

LUX

Calais

Agincourt
Crécy

Le Havre
Rouen
Amiens

Sedan
Reims

Versailles
Paris
Chartres
Orléans
Fontainebleau

Marne R.

Metz
Verdun
Nancy

Nantes

Loire R.

Tours

FRANCE

Poitiers

Bourges

Dijon

Strasbour

SWITZERLAND

Bordeaux

Clermont-Ferrand
Lascoux Cave

Vichy

Cluny

Lyons

Biarritz
Bayonne

Garonne R.

Saône R.

ITA

Carcassonne
Nîmes
Avignon
Arles
Marseilles

Rhône R.

MEDITERRANEAN SEA

Seine R.
Oise R.
Meuse R.
Rhine R.
Gironde R.

N

0   100

Scale of Miles

CORSICA

A CONCISE HISTORY OF

France

by Marshall B. Davidson

CASSELL • LONDON

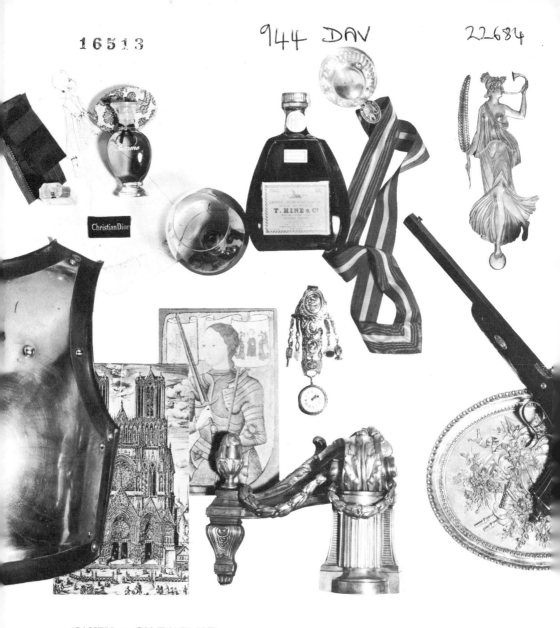

CASSELL & COMPANY LTD
35 Red Lion Square, London WC1R 4SJ
Sydney, Auckland, Toronto, Johannesburg

First published in Great Britain 1972
(I.S.B.N. 0 304 29000 9)
Manufactured in the United States of America

CHAPTER I

FROM CAVE DWELLERS
TO ROMAN CITIZENS

rance lies about midway between the Arctic Circle and the Equator. It is a temperate and a fecund land that for long centuries has been tilled and tended with devoted care, down to the very margins of its roadsides. Shortly before the birth of Christ the Greek geographer Strabo wrote that Gaul, the area roughly approximating today's France, seemed designed by nature to accommodate the various needs and wants of man. Two thousand years later, reviewing the history of the land, we can see how amply that promise has been fulfilled.

Viewed from the air, France resembles an irregular hexagon that is itself largely a design of nature; five sides of that rough shape are formed by the natural boundaries of sea and mountain. On the eastern and southwestern sides France is rimmed by the formidable, snow-capped ranges of the Alps and the Pyrenees respectively. Between those two high barriers the land opens out onto the Mediterranean along an inviting and picturesque coastline that stretches from the frontier of Italy on the east to that of Spain on the west. The fourth side of the hexagon sweeps in a large arc fronting the Atlantic and extending from the country's westernmost boundary with Spain to the tip

A bull from the wall paintings by primitive artists at the Lascaux Cave

of Brittany, reaching well out into the sea. In the northwest the coast-line of France runs roughly parallel to England's across the Channel. And, finally, on the northern frontier, angling inland to the east and back toward the Alps along the upper Rhine, France touches Belgium and Germany along a man-made and most sensitive boundary line.

As nations go, France is not large—less than a fourth the size of its former colony Algeria, somewhat larger than Spain, and, as one fur-ther measure, considerably smaller than the state of Texas. Within its modest bounds, however, the nation includes a number of distinct re-gions, each with its own physical character, its separate lore and tradi-tions, and in a few cases, notably Provence, Brittany, and the Basque portion of the Pyrenees, even its own regional language. Those dif-ferent areas might almost be thought of as countries within a country, and in the past some were indeed more or less independent dukedoms, princedoms, and kingdoms, occasionally at war with one another and with the anointed king of France, until they were finally brought to-gether under a single rule.

Taken as a whole, France displays a greater variety of natural fea-tures than can be found in virtually any other European country—lush river valleys, wooded hills, fertile plains, marshes, mountains, and varied shorelands; a fact that has played a significant part in French history. Over the millenniums, before and since Strabo's description, those diverse and agreeable aspects of the land have attracted settlers and plunderers, migrants and conquerors, merchants and adventurers, from all quarters of the Continent and beyond. Their path was made easier by the rivers that lead into the country from every direction and that form a weblike pattern of waterways spread over the land.

Unlike most countries of Europe, France has had the rare advan-tage of direct outlets both to the ancient world of the Mediterranean, with all its storied heritage of wealth and wisdom, and to the modern world that opened on the Atlantic, with all its new discoveries and unlimited horizons. And as opportunities beckoned in the course of history, access to either outlook could be quickly found up and down those interlocking rivers. Through such channels, also, came hordes from the North, hungry for the sun and the warmth, the glamour and the treasure of the more civilized Southern worlds. Other peoples moved up from the South along ancient trade routes to traffic in com-

This elaborately coiffed woman's head was fashioned in ivory some 24,000 years ago in the Les Landes region of western France.

modities from the North, and to linger and settle in the fertile valleys beyond the Alps. In time, the passage of immigrants and visitors made the country a major crossroads of the world, a place where stimulating and civilizing influences from every direction mingled and matured, and ultimately endowed the nation with a cultural importance out of all proportion to its limited size. Frenchmen are today a composite of the many different strains that have found their way into the country from elsewhere over the centuries.

The story of the French people begins with the story of man; that is, with the emergence in Europe of *Homo sapiens* during the fourth and last Ice Age. Those "sapient" men, probably migrants from the East, were the first known representatives of the human race, and they gradually replaced the Neanderthal men of still earlier ages. Like their predecessors, the newcomers were essentially cave men—cave dwellers or cave users—who hunted game and gathered food as best they could, but who produced nothing themselves. They were, in short, parasites and savages; contemporaries of the mammoth, the woolly rhinoceros, and other creatures now long extinct, and contenders with them for existence in what was then a hostile environment. Nevertheless, in their physical and mental potential they were little different from ourselves. (One branch of the early *sapiens,* the Cro-Magnons, were athletic, relatively handsome six-footers.) They were unacquainted with metals, but with flint and other tools they were capable of shaping bone, ivory, amber, and hard stones—as well as more perishable materials—into convincing and suggestive images. And with various pigments they reproduced the forms of living creatures on the rough walls of their caves for their own occult purposes.

Most likely the majority of the men who created such figures and designs were "professional" artists. They were perhaps the first specialists in history, individuals who were relieved of other duties within the community because of the importance placed upon their particular contributions. (It has even been suggested, somewhat extravagantly, that there may have been primitive "academies" where they were trained for their special work.) At any rate, their contributions must have served the common purposes of a group, although precisely what those purposes may have been can only be guessed.

We are considering here what is termed the Old Stone Age, or as archaeologists call it, the Upper Paleolithic period, very roughly between 30,000 and 10,000 B.C. This was long before the birth of ancient Egypt, and it covers a span of years far longer than the duration of Egypt's whole dynastic history—ten times longer than the time that separates our own day from the birth of Christ. It was toward the end of that long stretch, between about 15,000 and 10,000 B.C., that this very early Paleolithic art came to an astonishing climax in the lifelike renderings of wild beasts, the game and the predators whose habits the artists knew so well; notably in those paintings that can still be seen on the walls of the cave at Lascaux in southwestern France, and at a number of comparable sites.

During those passing centuries the very face of France (and the rest of Europe to be sure) was changing. At last the Ice Age was ending and, as the glaciers melted, the bleak steppes and tundras that had for so long conditioned the life of man were covered over by forests and other forms of vegetation. Different breeds of animals moved into this new habitat, and men of different culture—again probably migrants from the East—who were equipped to cope with those changing circumstances. The Old Stone Age was dissolving into the New Stone Age; the Paleolithic, through a transitional period, into the Neolithic; and the savages of earlier years were being replaced by the barbarians of the succeeding phase. Man changed from a parasite to a food producer, a herdsman and a farmer. He was on his way to being civilized.

Several millenniums before Christ, the first known architectural constructions in France were raised, those mysterious, impressive arrangements of giant stone slabs, known as dolmens, cromlechs, and menhirs, that can still be seen at Carnac and other sites on the Brittany peninsula. They are contemporaries and equivalents, presumably, of the carefully engineered constructions at Stonehenge, across the Channel in England. How such huge, enormously heavy stones were quarried, transported, and put in place can hardly be imagined. Some weighed hundreds of tons and one, now fallen, stood seventy feet high. Well-organized group effort was obviously required for their placement, and that the resulting structures served some religious purposes seems most likely. They are only rough shapes, but they appear to be everlasting. What fantastic ceremonies attended their installation we may never know. They are France's earliest standing monuments, rude and dis-

Over five feet high, this sixth-century B.C. *bronze wine vessel of Greek workmanship was recently found in a Celtic tomb at Vix, in Burgundy.*

tant ancestors of the great Gothic cathedrals that would rise from the landscape more than a score of centuries later.

Those extraordinary megalithic constructions were also, in a sense, memorials to the waning Age of Stone. With the introduction of metals—copper, then bronze, and finally iron—for tools, weapons, and other gear, in replacement of stone, man took a giant step in the march of civilization. Copper alone is too soft to provide a sharp and durable cutting edge or a strong, unyielding surface, but alloyed with tin it becomes bronze, which has those properties. When the formula for that alloy was revealed, the pace of life in France quickened, as it had in other lands to the east where such techniques had earlier been mastered. The tin of Cornwall and the copper of Spain were both within easy reach, and some time in the second millennium before Christ the Bronze Age dawned over western Europe.

It turned out to be a relatively brief, interim stage of development, for when the superior qualities of iron were realized in the following centuries, that metal assumed commanding importance. For those who knew its secrets and its strengths, iron was a formidable asset. France was liberally endowed with deposits of iron ore and with wood to burn for smelting it, and during the centuries that immediately preceded the Christian era what was forged from those resources played an important part in the economy and the destiny of the land. Yet again the pace of life accelerated, and it was even further quickened by the introduction of the horse and the wheel. The combined effect of the several developments was in the nature of a major revolution.

Just who were the "Frenchmen" of those years, very roughly the thousand years before Christ, is a tantalizing question. They left no written records; the first accounts of them are in the annals of the Greeks and the Romans, who knew them as northern neighbors—and as customers and adversaries. In the sixth century B.C. there was a Greek colony known as Massilia, or Marseilles, which a contemporary historian mentioned as lying in the country of the Ligurians close to the land of the Celts, and from which base the Greeks penetrated that land to establish trading colonies where Arles and Avignon now stand, along with other posts farther north. In 1953, near Châtillon in the heart of Burgundy, a colossal sculptured bronze vase of Greek workmanship and dating from the time of Croesus in the sixth century B.C.

was unearthed from the tomb of a Celtic princess. No bronze object at the same time so huge and so magnificent has been recovered from Greece itself or any of its ancient colonies. How such a treasure from the classical world reached that distant inland site, and why it was sent there, has not been explained; but it does suggest the enterprise of Greek traders. It could have been part of the tribute paid to a barbarian tribe that controlled the trade routes to the North.

The Ligurians and another people, the Iberians, both only hazily identified, also occupied areas of France. But the hinterland was then largely in the hands of those Celts, or Gauls as the Romans called them. While Greece and then Rome were spreading out in the Mediterranean world during the several centuries before the Christian era, Celtic tribes, erupting from the east, had swept over much of northern Europe and, wherever they could, made thralls of the various peoples they had found there. A Greek writer of the fourth century termed them one of the four great barbarian powers of the world.

Even earlier the Gauls had invaded Italy and sacked Rome (a minor city-state at the time), as they were shortly afterward to invade Greece with their horse-drawn wagons, war chariots, and great iron swords, and to sack Delphi. Some Celts moved on to what is now Turkey and settled in the region to be named Galatia. In time the Celts were overpowered and repulsed in Italy; in 124 B.C. Romans marched into Provence, a region inhabited by the "Gauls beyond the Alps"; and midway in the next century Julius Caesar undertook the campaign that brought all Gaul under Roman rule.

Caesar's conquest of Gaul was relatively swift and easy. The Celts were fierce warriors, but they had never formed an organized army, let alone a unified nation. They were a very loose conglomerate of tribes, frequently at war with one another, who imposed their authority and their culture—or tried to do so—on other barbarian peoples as they fought their way from the Danube across the breadth of France and beyond. In their internecine wars some of those tribes welcomed the support of Roman legions, now grown formidable; others sought such help to stem the assaults of the German hordes who threatened them from the north and east. Still others fought back at the Roman intruders, but their resistance was finally crushed with the defeat of their heroic leader Vercingetorix by Caesar in 52 B.C.

When that young chieftain, ceremoniously clad in gold-studded armor and handsomely mounted as if for parade, finally threw down his arms before his victor, all serious opposition on the part of the Gauls was ended. The Pax Romana, the Roman Peace, superseded anarchy and intertribal strife, and the rapid Romanization of Gaul proceeded with little further interruption. Over the several centuries to come, Gaul, in fact, became more Roman than Rome itself. Roman colonization policy was permissive and liberal, and for the most part the Gauls were eager enough to identify themselves with the prestigious empire that for a time yet promised the benefits, the material advances and the cultural rewards, of a highly civilized society and an orderly rule—even if that did mean paying taxes. The Gauls discarded their distinctive breeches for Roman togas and cropped their long hair in the Roman style, as did the Romanized Britons across the Channel; they gave themselves and their cities Roman names.

Gaul's Roman conquerors erected this municipal arch at Les Antiques, near the present-day town of Saint-Rémy, in Provence.

In France today one cannot go far without finding tangible evidences of that eager adoption of Roman ways. Provence, Rome's first southern province in Gaul, is of course studded with well-preserved and restored monuments from the classical period, such as the celebrated Pont du Guard at Nîmes and, nearby, the precious Maison Carrée, the little temple at which Thomas Jefferson gazed so long and lovingly in the eighteenth century and which inspired his design for the Virginia State Capitol; the amphitheater at Arles; the theater and triumphal arch at Orange; and so on down a long list.

Throughout the rest of France there is an abundance of other such venerable reminders of an ancient past. In numerous French museums one can see examples of the colorful mosaic floors that once adorned the baths and other public places as well as the Roman-style private villas that were scattered about the countryside, where men of means worked their ample estates. Most centers of any consequence had amphitheaters for the performance of gladiatorial games and other diversions. Even such a minor provincial town as Paris, earlier known as Lutetia (Lutèce), had its arena, which can still be seen there. It was relatively small as such structures went, yet it could seat ten thousand spectators. Also in Paris, adjoining the present Cluny Museum, stands the remains of the great Roman baths that measured more than one hundred yards across. Nearby, the present rue Saint-Jacques and the rue Saint-Martin follow the routes of early Roman highways leading south and west. The well-known boulevard Saint-Michel that slants across the Left Bank of Paris was in ancient times another, minor element in the network of solidly paved roads that was spread out across the breadth of Roman Gaul, stone arteries that fed new life to the entire land and shortened the way to Rome itself.

In the end, the acquisition of Gaul was a profoundly important move in the course of Roman empire. By pushing its frontier from the Alps to the Rhine, Rome had brought within its boundaries millions of hardy people; people who provided new markets for Roman commerce, who supplied large numbers of men for the armed services, and who invigorated the stock of the Roman population at a time when such a "booster" was becoming necessary for the survival of the Empire. Long before the end of the Empire, the legions protecting its frontiers from the barbarians in the north and northeast were almost entirely recruited from Gaul; the senators who sat at Rome included Gauls; Gauls served as consuls; the Gauls even wore the imperial purple. In the first century A.D. Claudius, a native of Lyons (then called Lugdunum), became emperor and extended the right of Roman citizenship and other privileges to many of his fellow townsmen in a pronouncement that was engraved on enduring bronze tablets. A century later, Caracalla, another Lyonnais, became emperor. "Caracalla" was in fact a nickname, derived from the long Gallic tunic he wore and that he introduced into the army. It was Caracalla, formally called Marcus Aurelius Antoninus, who accorded the rights of citizenship to all freeborn people throughout the Roman Empire.

As a footnote to the history of Roman Gaul, in A.D. 355 Julian, to be known as the Apostate, was proclaimed emperor of all Rome by his grateful troops on the Île de la Cité in the heart of what is now Paris. The next imperial coronation to be held at Paris was in 1804, almost a millennium and a half later, when Napoleon Bonaparte assumed the burdens of empire in a ceremony at the cathedral of Notre Dame. Between those two dates, through ages that were both dismally dark and splendidly brilliant, the French nation took on the shape and character that we are familiar with today.

CHAPTER II

THE DARKNESS
OF BARBARISM

*G*aul remained a Roman province for about five hundred years, from Caesar's conquest until the western Roman Empire collapsed in A.D. 476. That was as long a period as separates our own day from the discoveries of Columbus, and for most of those years Gaul flourished as a consequence of its attachment to the Empire. For more than three centuries the Pax Romana kept the land relatively tranquil. It was freer both from internal disruptions and from invasions than it ever would be again for so long a time. Gallic villages were developed into Roman cities of size and importance. As a prime example, Lyons, at the confluence of the Rhone and the Saône rivers and the starting point of four great roads, became a hub of traffic and commerce for the Western world. (Paris did not rise to comparable eminence for some time to come.) Industries and agriculture prospered, serving and profiting from the demands and needs of the central Roman state. Money became a common medium in the exchanges of merchants and traders, and a convenient form of investment. The Roman language and the Roman law, like the Roman roads, became binding ties that established a spirit of unity within a European empire, a unity that would continue

A fourteenth-century likeness of Charlemagne in silver and gold

to haunt the imagination of Frenchmen. It was a period that was recalled with nostalgia long after the dissolution of the Roman Empire. Centuries later Charlemagne dreamed of restoring some such unity to the bulk of the Continent. And a thousand years after that, in the age of Napoleon, the dream was again revived, only to turn into a nightmare of slaughter, rapine, and widespread distress.

Rome did not fall in a day, or in a century. The imperial machinery only gradually lost its power to hold together, to integrate, and to serve the vast and complex society of Roman peoples until it finally broke down altogether and left the Western world to darkness, and to outlandish folk who surged virtually at will across the old frontiers of empire and spread out across the land.

Such barbarian invasions were not so much a cause as a symptom of Rome's declining power. Actually, the invaders came not to destroy Roman civilization but to share its benefits. Since before the time of Caesar restless Germanic tribes beyond the Rhine had been viewing with envy the prospects from the other side of the river. In the beginning they infiltrated as enlistments to the Roman army, and as such they were welcome enough, for as Tacitus wrote, they made brave and dedicated warriors, always willing to spill blood—even the blood of their own or neighboring tribesmen if Rome required it.

By the fourth century entire tribes of Germans were serving as mercenaries and allies in the Roman army; allies who occasionally took matters in their own hands, elected their own commanders, and swept over Gaul to get what they wanted from that coveted land, from the Rhine to the Pyrenees. Other Germanic tribes, looking for fresh land and living space, entered Gaul to serve as buffer colonies against still more barbarians who were pushing on from the north and east. In the fifth century such migrants came in great hordes that spread out over the entire face of Gaul, and beyond Gaul into Spain and Italy. With their numbers they swamped the Gallo-Romans. Gaul was now their land to hold and nurture as best they could.

To describe the complex interrelationships of the numerous Germanic tribes who accomplished this take-over would be wearisome. It suffices to recall the names of some of them. There were Goths—Ostrogoths (Goths of the East) and Visigoths (Goths of the West); there were Alamanni, Burgundians, Lombards, and Vandals; and there were

Franks (the Ripuarian Franks from the riverbanks and the Salian Franks from the salt lands), who in time would give the name France to what had so long been known as Gaul. And behind them were the Huns, storming out of Asia, whose ferocity and ruthlessness made even the Germans blanch with terror and sent them fleeing into Gaul for refuge. In the middle of the fifth century, under their warrior-leader Attila, aptly called the Scourge of God, the Huns turned away from the gates of Constantinople and themselves surged into Gaul, driving more Germans before them—those who could escape—as the eastern hordes advanced.

The city of Metz was destroyed in that charge, but Paris was spared. According to legend, Geneviève, a saintly virgin of that city, heartened the inhabitants by assuring them Attila would be diverted, as he was, and in grateful memory of her trust and suasion, she is revered as the patron saint of the city to this day. But the Huns passed on to besiege Orléans. Then, in 451, at Châlons, a motley army of Visigoths, Franks, and Burgundians under the command of a Roman official named Aëtius fought and defeated the Huns and those Ostrogoths, Franks, and Burgundians who had joined Attila's ranks. For the most part it was barbarian against barbarian. Attila withdrew, carried on his pillage in Italy, and finally disappeared from history altogether. The Germans left to piece together as best they could the remnants of Roman Gaul.

In the slow, often agonizing re-formation of Roman Gaul into the kingdom of France the Christian Church played a very important role, and an extremely difficult one. Christianity had been introduced into the land as early as the first century A.D. by traveling merchants who spread the "good news" of Christ's Gospel as they peddled their wares. In Gaul as elsewhere in the old Empire the new religion at first suffered frightful persecutions. To the delight of pagan spectators, subscribers to the Christian faith were thrown to wild beasts in the arenas, among other torments they were put to. But persecution only added strength to the growing community of believers, and soon the Roman state—which is to say the emperors—found it expedient to tolerate that community. The Empire, it seemed, would need such indomitable adherents. In the fourth century Christianity was even granted imperial favor. By the time the barbarian invasions approached high tide, Gaul was on its way to being Christianized.

Thus, somewhat earlier in Paris, around A.D. 250, a Christian missionary named Denis had his head chopped off because his proselytizing zeal offended those who worshiped other gods. But he picked it up, we are told, and carried it in his arms until he found nearby his eternal resting place. Within three centuries a Christian basilica was raised over the site, seven miles north of the center of Paris, to glorify his martyrdom. Denis became the patron saint of France, and the monastery of Saint-Denis, dedicated to his memory, became the richest and most important in the country—the burial place for kings and queens, princes, and nobles of the realm in years to come. The hilltop where Denis had been murdered, the highest point in what is now the city of Paris and a place that had been sacred to the pagan god Mercury, became known as the Mount of the Martyrs, or Montmartre, noted more recently for its cafés and night life.

Hardly more than a century after the martyrdom of Denis, an ex-soldier named Martin, converted to Christianity after he had given half of his cloak to a beggar at Amiens and thereupon had a vision, won such prodigious fame by evangelizing the countryside and organizing its religious life that today hundreds of French towns and thousands of French churches still carry his name. By the time of his death, about A.D. 400, Christianity was firmly established in all the influential quarters of the land. As the barbarians advanced the Church was becoming the heir and representative of the old Roman culture—a guide and teacher to the newcomers to civilization. To effect its works the Church developed an organization that closely followed and gradually replaced that of the fading imperial system, directed on the same general principles and with the same structure as the civil administration. Each city had its bishop, civil provinces came under the jurisdiction of ecclesiastical archbishops and metropolitans, and so on. The framework of a new unity, based on different loyalties and subject to novel conditions, had been built.

To bring the various German tribes that had staked their separate claims within Gaul into that unity of the orthodox was a supreme test. The barbarians were not averse to accepting Christianity, or rather to identifying their tribal gods with the Christian saints as they had earlier identified or confused them with the Roman gods. But they viewed the new faith with differing concepts, and they warred among themselves.

Saint Martin of Tours is shown converting a band of thieves to Christianity in this fifteenth-century embroidery.

The most important single episode in the religious struggle that followed was the conversion of Clovis, king of the Salian Franks, in 496. Clovis swore to his Christian wife (the only Christian princess in Gaul) that if her god would help him defeat the Alamanni in battle, he would consent to be baptized. Clovis (a name which was to become Louis) was indeed victorious and he kept his word, whereupon three thousand of his warriors followed his lead. The king was baptized and anointed with holy oil by the bishop of Reims, a gesture that for centuries to come was to give divine sanction to the French monarchy.

With Clovis' victory the reunification of Roman-Gallic territory as the Frankish kingdom was begun. Also, the alliance of that kingdom with the Church was established, a liaison that laid the foundations of medieval history. In 507 Clovis launched a great campaign against the Goths who had settled on the land to the south, between the Loire River and the Pyrenees. It was, in fact, a Christian crusade, for the Goths held to unorthodox doctrines. "With God's help," Clovis is said to have announced, "let us go and conquer them and take their territories." That he did, accompanied by miraculous signs of divine favor. And with that further victory a new Catholic state took form in the West—a state that with other, quickly following Frankish conquests spread eastward across the Rhine. At Constantinople the Eastern emperor, Anastasius, recognized Clovis' authority and conferred upon him the insignia of a Roman magistrate. The Christian Frankish chief had taken the place of the ancient emperors in the Western world— and he chose Paris as the most strategic spot for his capital. With these circumstances it might be said that the French nation was conceived.

The line of kings beginning with Clovis is known as the Merovingian dynasty, so called after Clovis' grandfather, Merovaeus, a chief of great renown who had fought with Aëtius against the Huns. The Merovingians ruled for about two and a half centuries. A detailed recital of what happened during those years makes dismal and confused reading. In brief outline, the sons of Clovis added to their father's conquests over the other German tribes who had laid claims to portions of Roman Gaul. Burgundy and Provence were brought under Frankish dominion. But the brothers contended for supremacy among themselves, as did their heirs and successors for generations to come. No rule or tradition dictated the direct transfer of supreme power from one individual to

With head in hands, the martyred Saint Denis seeks his heavenly home.

another. Each son inherited his share of the kingdom and did what he could about it.

The principle of unity that Clovis had so closely approached was shattered by fratricidal strife that amounted to bloody chaos. Unmentionable atrocities became almost commonplace in the round of royal maneuvers. And in the process the Merovingian kings became so decadent and debauched that they could no longer master their own minions. As the prestige of the monarch declined, authority over the affairs of state, such as they were, was assumed by officials known as Mayors

of the Palace, who had charge of the kingly estates and households and who engaged in their own rivalries.

By the middle of the seventh century it seemed likely that the kingdoms of the Merovingians, "that bankrupt and accursed house" as a later chronicler called it, would remain split into eternally warring fragments. What hope there was for a peaceful, Christian rule and a settled society almost vanished altogether when, early in the next century, the crusading warriors of Islam came storming over the Pyrenees in the course of their holy war to proselytize the world in the name of Mohammed. It had taken them a mere seven years to conquer Spain, whither the Visigoths had retreated before the Franks under Clovis (and it would take eight centuries to win back that land completely in the name of Christ). They burned with zeal, these Moslems, or Moors as they were called, although they were a mixed horde of Arabs and Africans alike. After occupying Narbonne, in the south of France, in 719, and extorting ransom from Nîmes, they moved on up the Rhone valley to destroy the city of Autun; they captured Bordeaux near the southwest coast and forced their way to Tours, where Saint Martin had been bishop three centuries earlier, in the gardenlike valley of the Loire River.

These were no ordinary invaders. Fighting a holy cause, they had for a century past swept over Asia and Africa, from the Indian Ocean to the Atlantic, overcoming all opposition. As they reached the heartland of France they seemed invincible. Then, in 732 at a site between Tours and Poitiers, these ferocious horsemen from the east were met by a Frankish force brought together by Charles Martel, a bastard mayor of the palace and an able military leader who had recently prevailed over the other mayors to become, in effect, ruler of the Franks. ("Martel" was actually an apt nickname meaning "hammer.") And there the Moors, or Saracens, as they are also called, were finally thrown back—their first decisive defeat in a century of overriding triumphs across half the world. (It was precisely one hundred years after the death of Mohammed.) Had it not been so, wrote Edward Gibbon in the eighteenth century, scholars at Oxford would then have been expounding on the Koran to a circumcised Europe—a curious but evocative speculation that dramatizes that turning point in history.

However extravagant Gibbon's speculation may have been, the vic-

Saracen soldiers, united under the banner of Islam, prepare to fight their Christian foes.

tory of Charles Martel over the Moslems and his other conquests over divided elements within the Frankish kingdom gave that mayor such power as no individual had known since the days of Clovis—power that was concentrated and enhanced by his son and successor, called Pepin the Short. In 751 Pepin, with the assent of the beleaguered pope in Rome, who sorely needed his military support against the assaults of Lombard tribes, cut off the royal locks of the last of the Merovingian kings and sent him off to a monastery. By the acclaim of a great assembly of his liegemen Pepin was elected king of the Franks. The pope solemnified the election in 754 by anointing Pepin at the abbey church of Saint-Denis in Paris, conferring upon him the additional title of Patrician of the Romans.

That nomination was actually the legal prerogative of the Eastern emperor in Constantinople, still the nominal head of the ancient Roman Empire. By taking the matter in his own hands, the pope cut his ties with that traditional authority and cast his lot with the Western monarchy as his support and protector. In return, Pepin's armies twice crossed the Alps and forced the Lombards to cede the territory stretching between Rome and Ravenna (lands which were the legitimate possessions of the emperor at Constantinople), which Pepin in turn gave to the pope, thus founding the temporal power of the papacy that endured for more than eleven hundred years—until 1870.

When the pope had earlier journeyed at great travail across the Alps to Saint-Denis to anoint Pepin, for good measure he also anointed Pepin's two sons, the twelve-year-old Charles and his brother Carloman, thus gracing them also with royal prerogatives. Carloman died three years after his father, and Charles, known to history as Charlemagne (that is, Carolus Magnus, or Charles the Great), became sole ruler of the large kingdom that had been consolidated by Pepin. At twenty-nine he was indisputably the strongest ruler of western Europe, a figure who grew in majesty during his lifetime and who became a legendary figure, much larger than life, after his death. He was remembered as the "Emperor with the Flowery Beard" (no verifiable portrait of him remains, but apparently he was clean shaven, or at most had only a mustache), gigantic in size (his skeleton indicated that he was, in fact, about six feet four inches tall), and two hundred years old (he died at the age of seventy-two)—a man who was held in awe from

Britain to Baghdad—an invincible Christian conqueror, inspired by angels, whose sword *Joyeuse* had contained the point of the lance used in the Passion. Some said he would arise from the dead, others that he did indeed do so to join the Crusades. He was credited with miraculous powers and implausible virtues. In the twelfth century he was canonized, and until recent times the Day of Saint Charlemagne, the "inventor of schools," was a cherished holiday for French school children.

But however extraordinary their growth, the legends about Charlemagne were rooted in historical realities, and these, even in the most factual chronicles, often have an epic quality that challenges the imagination. For more than thirty years Charlemagne warred in all directions, until his dominions stretched from the Mediterranean to the North Sea, and from the Atlantic to the Elbe and the lower Danube. He finally subdued the Lombards in Italy, he virtually obliterated the Avars, those savage mounted nomads from the Eurasian steppes, and in eighteen campaigns he overcame the fierce Saxons of the North, forcing baptism on those who survived his murderous charges (4,500 of them were hanged in a single day). In 778 he launched an ill-fated offensive against the Saracens in Spain; he was obliged to retreat across the Pyrenees. This was, nevertheless, his most celebrated campaign. The legend that grew from it, as later imaginatively told in the *Chanson de Roland,* became one of the greatest epic tragedies of history.

It is tempting to dwell on Charlemagne, for he is one of the three great heroes, along with Caesar and Napoleon, who have at separate times held sway over most of the European continent. The climax of his career came when, at Rome on Christmas Day A.D. 800, the pope crowned him the first Holy Roman Emperor. More than eight centuries had passed since Caesar's conquest of Gaul. But the conviction that the Roman Empire still existed faded very slowly. In spite of the violence and cruelty with which Charlemagne imposed his rule on Europe, men were beginning again to sense anew the blessings of the Pax Romana. Charlemagne did try to revive the ideals of classical antiquity, in a Christian context. Alcuin, the famous English scholar who was the emperor's adviser in educational and religious matters and the principal intellect in what is called the Carolingian Renaissance, told the emperor that in the land of the Franks there might be reared "a new Athens enriched by the sevenfold fullness of the Holy Spirit."

Charlemagne accomplished both more and less than that. He did not succeed in reviving the glory and the grandeur of the classical past, and he did not manage to bring a peaceful and unified rule to Western Christendom. But in his tireless efforts to attain those ends he gave spur to other developments of momentous importance. For untold centuries the shores of the Mediterranean had mothered a succession of great civilizations; the ancient cities of Athens, Alexandria, Rome, and Byzantium had nourished the growth of man's most progressive and creative spirit. But those centers had lost the dynamism that had made them great in the past, and when Charlemagne constructed his vast empire and gathered to his court the scholars and scribes, the artists and craftsmen who gave it luster, he shifted the center of cultural ferment in Europe up into the heartland of the Franks' rural dominions—to a land that had shortly before been identified only with long northern nights, dark forests, and the unfamiliar ways of outlandish folk. Here, beyond the Alps, would be forged an amalgam of the highly disparate traditions of both Northern and Southern worlds. And from that fusion a new society and a new civilization would ultimately emerge.

For all his indomitable energy, Charlemagne was mortal. It is told that at the end of his career he was accompanied on all his royal progresses by an elephant, Abu-l-Abbas by name, a prized gift from the caliph Harun al-Rashid, who was to be immortalized in *The Arabian Nights*. When Abu died on one of Charlemagne's last campaigns against the Danes, it was deemed an omen of darkest portent. The campaign was indeed indecisive and the emperor himself died three years later, in 814. Within a few generations the great empire he had so laboriously pieced together was already a shambles.

In his later years the aging emperor is said to have wept at the thought of the menacing advances of Vikings along the northern and western perimeters of his realm. Now, ever more boldly, the dreaded longboats with their high dragon prows were slipping up the Seine, the Loire, and other convenient waterways, spreading terror and destroying every vestige of imperial authority wherever their raids reached. In 843 they killed the bishop of Nantes before his high altar and a few years later burned the church of Saint-Martin at Tours; Paris itself was sacked in 845. Meanwhile, Saracens attacked Rome and violated Saint Peter's, nomadic hordes of Magyars pressed in from the east. Charle-

IRELAND

York •

ENGLAND

London •
Canterbury •

NORTH SEA

BALTIC SEA

SAXONY

Elbe R.

Aachen •

AUSTRASIA
• Mainz

EAST

FRANKISH

KINGDOM

Danube R.

BRITANNY

NEUSTRIA

WEST

⚔ Tours

Luxeuil •

Rhine R.

Strasbourg

SWABIA

BAVARIA

FRANKISH

AQUITAINE

BURGUNDY

• St. Gall

Rhone R.

KINGDOM

⚔ Roncevalles

SPANISH MARCH

• Barcelona

KINGDOM
• Bobbio

OF

PAPAL STATES

⚔ Ravenna

ITALY

CORSICA

• Rome

SPAIN

• Monte
Cassino

DUCHY OF
BENEVENTO

AVARS

SARDINIA

CHARLEMAGNE'S EMPIRE

Charlemagne's empire, 814

Tributary states under Charlemagne

TREATY OF VERDUN, 843

••••••• Area east of this line went to Louis

━ ━ ━ Area west of this line went to Charles
Italy and area between lines went to Lothair

TREATY OF MERSEN, 870

━━━ Division of East and West Frankish Kingdoms

MEDITERRANEAN SEA

SICILY

*A map showing the division of Charlemagne's vast dominions shortly after his
death in A.D. 814, including more than half of Europe*

magne's heirs were incapable of maintaining even a semblance of political unity within the crumbling Empire. Once again Europe divided into a dismal miscellany of contending and often hostile forces.

The centuries immediately following Charlemagne's death—the ninth and tenth—may fairly be called a dark age. But even in that gloom can be discerned important events that forecast the shape of things to come. In 842 two of the emperor's grandsons made an agreement of mutual support (in opposition to a third grandson), taking an oath that was issued in the vernacular commonly used by their armies —the first written examples of those dialects that would later develop into the French and German languages. In a treaty agreed to a year later, the three brothers parceled out among them the territories from which would emerge the separate nations of France and Germany. The third, middle kingdom between those two areas was a long and somewhat loosely defined, curving strip of land that stretched from the Atlantic to the Mediterranean and that would serve as a battleground for those two incipient nations down to our own day. Meanwhile, the Carolingian line faded into obscurity like the Merovingian before it.

Early in the tenth century Charles the Simple, the Carolingian king whose territory comprised much of the France of today, had been obliged to concede to the invading Norsemen a large area on either side of the Seine River, downstream from Paris, where it flows westward to empty into the sea. The Norse pirates settled firmly on that land, to be known as Normandy, and within a short span of time became thoroughly naturalized Frenchmen in their manners, language, and institutions. They were Christianized and they ruled their province admirably.

In 987 the last of the enfeebled Carolingian kings died in an accident. For a century past the descendants of Charlemagne had actually occupied the throne only intermittently, alternating with members of the house of Robert the Strong, who were sometimes known as the Dukes of France. This family owned more land than the king himself, and its representatives were of stronger fiber. Thus it was one of them, Hugh Capet, who in that year 987 was elected by the great nobles of the land to be the sole and real king of the realm; and he was duly and solemnly anointed as such by the archbishop of Reims. Hugh, a great-grandson of Robert the Strong, assumed his surname Capet, it has been said, because he had been lay abbot of the old Gaulish sanctuary Saint-

Martin of Tours, where the cape of that great and holy man was kept as a most precious relic. The kingdom he acquired was by then a loose assemblage of discordant fragments, pieced together in the dark shadows of external pressures and internal strife. In the absence of any effective central authority, and in the face of general insecurity and of specific peril from marauding, anarchic forces, society was reduced to an elementary condition in which those who were strong protected those within a limited territory who were weak in exchange for other services rendered in return. Such personal relationships developed into the inexplicably complicated system of feudalism, which in the end bound the king, the servants of the Church, and every degree of knight and workman in an intricate web of fealties and courtesies, of obligations and payments, of exemptions and privileges. Actually, feudalism was anything but systematic. As has been said, it amounted to "confusion roughly organized." It was political and social organization reduced to the lowest terms.

The struggle of the French monarchy to overcome the contesting and divisive elements of the feudal order very briefly summarizes the history of France for centuries to come. For almost nine of those centuries, following the accession of Hugh, the house of Capet, the Capetians and its cadet branches, the Valois and the Bourbons, would provide the kings of the land, and under their rule modern France took lasting form. The great, consolidating achievements of the Capetians was to establish the rule of primogeniture, abrogating all past laws and customs but assuring the single, uncontested inheritance of the Crown by each eldest son in unbroken succession.

CHAPTER III

MEDIEVAL
CRUCIBLE

*U*ntil fairly recently the entire millennium between the fall of Rome and, let us say, the discovery of America—very roughly the years between 500 and 1500—was termed the Dark Ages. In the sixteenth century Rabelais described those thousand years as "the tenebrous and calamitous night of the Goths," and so others continued to see it. As already noted, there were times during the first half of that period, both before and after the reign of Charlemagne, when the outlook for civilization was indeed not bright; when barbarism and anarchy threatened to replace altogether the culture and settled order that had prevailed in France under Roman rule. It is one indication of the flux and uncertainties of those years that hardly a monument dating from that long period still stands in France. Recalling the abundance of monumental remains from the earlier, Roman period, and considering the great monasteries, cathedrals, fortresses, and town complexes that would rise in the several hundred years following A.D. 1000, those five hundred years do indeed seem like a dark void.

Yet, if we look elsewhere for evidence, we find more brilliance and skilled accomplishment in that period than is implied by the term Dark

Sainte-Chapelle, illuminated by its incomparable stained-glass windows

Ages. Barbarism is after all not savagery, but rather a degree or stage of social organization. (The Greek word *barbaros* meant "foreigner," and was first applied to the highly civilized Persians.) For us the word *barbarian* signifies a tribal culture rather than that of a settled, centrally organized state. The various tribes who entered France to settle there brought with them a rich heritage in their arts as in their folkways, traditions that were deeply rooted in a distant past. Like that of most nomadic peoples, however, their art was typically small in scale and portable—personal and military trappings, brooches, buckles, and weaponry—and it was ornamented with geometric and interlacing patterns, including a fantastic imagery of bestial motifs, an imagery completely alien to the spirit of classical antiquity, but one that had its own pronounced sophistication and a vigor that had been all but forgotten along Mediterranean shores.

Although the vast political empire Charlemagne had forged from the disparate and often discordant elements of Western society did not long survive his death, the fusion of various cultures continued. As those strains were gradually brought within the context of the Christian faith, the development of a coherent medieval Western civilization becomes apparent—a civilization that was rooted in and came to full flower in the central area of the old Frankish territory, most dramatically in northern France.

It was in the early dawn of that era that Hugh Capet was crowned king of the Franks. To some, however, those last decades of the tenth century seemed more like the fading twilight of the recent past. As the year 1000 drew near, in any case, an apocalyptic spirit, a "millennarian psychosis," revealed the underlying anxieties of the time. The Day of Judgment, so long ago prophesied, was held by some to be close at hand. At a council held in 991 the French bishops announced, "We seem to be witnessing the coming of Antichrist, for this is the falling away of which the Apostle [John] speaks." Yet the critical year came and went without extraordinary calamity, and as the new century dawned it began to seem that the world might, after all, have at least another thousand years to go. A fresh spirit of confidence was generated that was brightly reflected in art and architecture. "It was as if the whole earth, having cast off the old by shaking itself," wrote one chronicler in 1003, "were putting on a white robe of churches."

There were far more tangible reasons than the release from millennarian tensions, and more important reasons than the advent of the
Capetians, certainly, to account for the spirit of the new century. The
signs of revival were apparent before Hugh was anointed—well before
the turn of the tenth century, in fact—and they were not confined to
France. For long years the Church had been plagued by problems that
grew out of the barbarian invasion on the one hand and the decadence
of its own administration on the other. Charlemagne's efforts to reform
the Church by his imperial authority had proved abortive. In one letter
to the pope the emperor emphatically admonished him to "live honestly
and to give special attention to observing the holy canons," but his
strictures were not always heeded or obeyed.

Then, in the course of the tenth century, by a series of internal reforms and reorganizations, the ecclesiastical structure gathered new
strength. The single factor that lends unity to the next three centuries
was, indeed, the authority of the Christian Church, a binding force that
was felt not only in spiritual matters, but in art and literature, science
and law, politics and economics, and, if we recall the Crusades, even in
war. It was the Church, in the end, that achieved a consolidation of
medieval European culture, over which it sometimes exercised a militant authority—as when in 1077 Pope Gregory kept the Holy Roman
Emperor, Henry IV, waiting three days and three nights in the snow at
Canossa, "barefoot and clad only in a wretched woolen garment," before granting him absolution and forgiveness for his transgressions.
The history of France remained intimately and inseparably linked with
the history of the Church.

It was in the monasteries that the latent and powerful spirit of Christianity and the seed of learning that informed it had survived the violence of barbarian invasion that had stormed over Europe in the days
following Charlemagne; and it was in good measure through the
agency of the monasteries that the Church carried out its reforms and
made its influence felt. Of these monasteries the most important was
the one at Cluny, in French Burgundy. By papal decree the abbot of
Cluny was responsible only to Rome, and neither king nor bishop could
interfere in the management of the affairs of the order. It had the right
to coin special money. Cluny became, in fact, the headquarters of a
monastic empire that embraced virtually all Europe within its spiritual

jurisdiction; its emissaries carried the cultural influence along with the discipline of the order in all directions. At the height of its power Cluny controlled more than a thousand associated establishments spread as far apart as Scotland and Jerusalem. Gifts and legacies rained upon the order from all Europe. For almost half a millennium the abbey church at Cluny, today a sad but vastly impressive ruin (it was almost entirely demolished during the Napoleonic period), remained the largest and most sumptuous building in Christendom—that is, from around A.D. 1100, when it was built, until the new cathedral of Saint Peter was raised at Rome in the sixteenth century. So large and sumptuous was it, indeed, that Bernard of Clairvaux (head of a rival French monastic order and a reformer of austere stripe) felt obliged to remonstrate against the "immoderate" length, the "immense" height, and the "super-vacuous" width of the edifice, as well as against the "monstrous" imagery of its sculptures, the "costly polishings, and the curious carvings and paintings which attract the worshiper's gaze and hinder his attentions."

But Cluny was only the most imposing of the great churches that were rising throughout Europe, and nowhere more abundantly than in France. The various monastic orders encouraged pilgrimages of the faithful to the shrines of saints, the sanctuaries where relics of holy personages were treasured. And in the new churches that sprang into being at those sites, as though some magical stone seed had been sown across the land, the Romanesque style of art and architecture germinated and flowered into a fresh and astonishing creation in France. Christian art was entering the most glorious period of its history, as can still be seen in churches spread over the face of the country—at Mont-Saint-Michel, Vézelay, Autun, Toulouse, Conques, Caen, and on down a long list of glorious survivals, precursors of the even more resplendent Gothic cathedrals of the twelfth and thirteenth centuries.

For all its faults and its incentives to petty warfare, feudalism, along with the ecclesiastical organization (which was part of the feudal system), had maintained a degree of order and stability during a painful period of adjustment. By the eleventh century commercial activity had reawakened. Merchants followed the pilgrims' paths and turned them into trade routes. After centuries of steady decline urban life was revivified and wealth increased. Population was also increasing and not

Relief carvings from Autun Cathedral portray the three magi with their gifts for the Christ child.

only did old towns grow, but wholly new towns were founded by the Church, as by kings and nobles. The right of asylum and other special privileges were offered to settlers. (At least one enterprising cleric imported women as wives to gratify the men he had brought to his new settlement.) Those planned communities can still be traced in many of the place names in France that contain the phrase *ville neuve*—as Villeneuve-lès-Avignon, across the river from the old city of Avignon.

In this resurgence of spirit and enterprise the first Capetian kings played but a minor part. Compared to their powerful feudal neighbors and vassals—the duke of Normandy and the great counts of Flanders, Anjou, and Champagne—they controlled relatively little territory and commanded only limited force. They did however directly control the Île-de-France, and there, at Paris, for once and all they reinstated the capital of the kingdom. And it was about Paris that the French nation would take its shape.

But for the rest, what happened at the start of the dynasty was either against their will or without help from those kings of France. In 1066 William the Bastard, duke of Normandy, crossed the Channel to conquer England and become monarch of that island—and to take command of its resources. This vassal of the French king was both richer and more powerful than his suzerain, and Normandy became a dependency of England. (In passing, William urgently called for Cluniac monks to help strengthen his work and position in England, offering to pay for them with their weight in gold; but his bid was refused on the grounds that there was greater need for such emissaries elsewhere.) In the years to come the royal heirs and successors of William, with their allies, would challenge the kings of France for sovereignty over their hereditary dominions in long and sanguinary encounters. It was in the course of that conflict that Joan of Arc played her heroic role and became a fresh and enduring symbol of French nationhood.

With the end of that long, so-called Hundred Years' War in 1453, the Anglo-Norman pretenders lost their last serious claim to the French throne. It was one climactic moment in the old struggle of the kings of France to prevail over the divisive and anarchic forces of feudalism; a struggle that had its uncertain beginnings with the coronation of Hugh Capet and that, in the centuries following, would impose a lasting shape and structure on the French nation.

Although the first Capetian rulers accomplished little in this direction on their own initiative, their position was favored by circumstances they did not altogether control. However restricted their worldly authority may have been, from the beginning they were recognized—or, more truly, established—by the Church as the Lord's Anointed; a spiritual distinction that in an age of faith could not be altogether ignored by even the most powerful and contentious of the king's vassals.

Then, in 1095, a scant generation after the Norman conquest of England, the French-born, ex-Cluniac monk Pope Urban II delivered one of the most moving orations recorded in history at the town of Clermont-Ferrand in Auvergne, the mountainous central region of France. No building in that area was large enough to contain the audience that gathered to hear his message. In the open air, therefore, he addressed the huge assembly, praising the valor of the Franks, calling upon his listeners to remember the heroic deeds of their ancestors, and urging them to put aside their petty squabbles and civil strife at home and to take up arms against those infidels who were desecrating Christianity's most cherished shrines in the Holy Land. Such a departure, he counseled them, would be God's own work for which they would be rewarded on earth as in Heaven.

Thus was launched the First Crusade. The pope himself was surprised and almost embarrassed by the response to his exhortation. Even women, monks and priests, old men and children, rallied to the crusaders' banners and had to be restrained from marching off with and becoming a burden to the able-bodied warriors of fighting age. Among the latter were, quite naturally, some of the most aggressive and formidable feudal lords of the land. And while they were away the king, who wisely stayed at home, seized what opportunities he could find to bolster and enhance his royal prerogatives.

Although the crusading fervor rapidly spread to other countries, it was from the start a French phenomenon. The volunteer forces consisted largely of French knights, and in the Near East crusaders of whatever region were commonly termed "Franks" or, as their pillage and slaughter progressed, "arrogant and bloodthirsty Franks." At least some part of the intolerance associated with traditional Moslem attitudes toward the Christian world may have stemmed from the bloodshed visited on Moslems and Jews by those marauding Christian

knights from France and elsewhere in Europe. "If you desire to know
what was done with the enemy who were found there," it was reported
to the pope by the Christian hosts at Jerusalem, "know that in Solomon's Porch and in his temple our men rode in the blood of the Saracens up to the knees of their horses."

That was only the first of a series of crusades that were launched and
carried on over a period of about two centuries; a series of adventures
and misadventures in which the French continued to play a conspicuous
part. Violent as it often was, the contact of East and West broke down
old barriers and released an interchange of ideas and of goods that
vastly benefited the Western world in years to come. The Christians
had a great deal to learn from Islam, including a need they had not
earlier recognized (at least since Roman days) for silks and spices and
dyes, figs and fragrant oils and precious stones, all things that could be
funneled through the Near Eastern ports of the Mediterranean to the
Western world. In spite of the worst excesses that were perpetrated by
either side, there was fraternization and a measure of mutual respect
between the hostile forces. As one by-product of those years of inter-

*Krak des Chevaliers, in present-day Syria, was erected by French crusaders in
1136 in the architectural style of their homeland.*

mittent warfare, the principalities of the Holy Land were converted,
for a while, into exotic outposts of feudal France. There are castles in
Syria and a cathedral in Famagusta that would not be out of place in
Île-de-France. More importantly, the singular prestige enjoyed by
French culture throughout the Levant lasted for centuries to come. The
ill-starred French mandate over Syria and Lebanon between the past
two world wars was the unhappy last act of a drama that had begun in
turmoil almost nine hundred years earlier.

While the successive crusades were running their course, for reasons
only indirectly associated with those expeditions, France was develop-
ing into the strongest kingdom in Europe—what is more, into a monarchy in which the supremacy of the king was increasingly evident. The
capacity of the Capetian rulers to produce male heirs for generation
after generation, the eldest of whom was regularly acknowledged and
anointed by churchly authority, provided a continuity unprecedented
in the history of French royalty. However, for those royal heirs to recover the prerogatives that since the days of Charlemagne had been
usurped by other feudal lords, and to consolidate the large and scattered holdings of those often powerful rulers under the direct administration of the Crown, was a large and complicated task.

Yet, by patient maneuvering, by shrewdly planned marriages, by
occasional inheritances, by intrigue, by purchase, and by force of arms
this is what the Capetians largely accomplished over a period of somewhat more than three hundred years. At the time of his coronation in
987 Hugh Capet directly controlled only a tiny fraction of the territory
included in modern France—less than 2 per cent. His capital was not
fixed; with his court he moved from one fortified stronghold to another
as circumstances required. When the Capetian line came to an end in
1328, the royal domain was forty times larger, it had been provided
with the administrative machinery necessary for centralized government, and Paris had become the permanent capital of the nation and
the cultural and intellectual center of Europe—the Queen of Cities.

In the twelfth and thirteenth centuries the transformation of Paris
was remarkable. Offended by the noisome character of the city's streets,
Philip II (1180–1223), seventh of the fourteen Capetian rulers and
better known as Philip Augustus, had the principal thoroughfares of
Paris paved over for the first time in history. He gave the city a perma-

nent central market, situated on the site where Les Halles continued thus to serve Parisians until a very few years ago. About the year 1200, near the western border of the city, Philip built an impressive fortress known as the Louvre, remnants of which may still be seen amid the masonry of the enormous structure, bearing the same name, that in centuries to come grew from those early beginnings. During Philip's reign, as well, the great Gothic cathedral of Notre Dame, begun in 1163, rose in its majesty at the very heart of the city. (To this day all distances to other points in France are measured from the parvis, or open space in front of the portal of Notre Dame.) And there were other churches, hospitals, an aqueduct, and still more constructions and improvements that decisively changed the face of Paris. In 1243–46 Philip's grandson, Saint Louis, built the exquisitely beautiful Sainte-Chapelle, barely a long stone's throw from Notre Dame, to house those relics of inestimable value that he had garnered during his crusading days in the East—notably the precious object believed to be the Crown of Thorns. (Shortly after Louis acquired that treasure at enormous cost, another "Crown of Thorns" became available to the highest bidder.) Almost miraculously, that architectural jewel with its fifty-foot-high stained-glass windows, incorporating more than a thousand scenes from the Old Testament, the Gospels, and the Apocalypse, remains virtually intact today.

Gothic art and architecture, so memorably represented by those two Parisian examples, was essentially a French creation; more specifically, a creation of the Île-de-France, homeland of the Capetians. From there the Gothic style rapidly spread within France and then throughout much of Europe, from Spain to Sweden. History has rarely witnessed such an extraordinary outburst of creative activity. "In the single century between 1170 and 1270," wrote Henry Adams, with wonder, "the French built eighty cathedrals and nearly five hundred churches of the cathedral class . . . and this covered only the great churches of a single century." Happily, the French countryside today still bears ample witness to that remarkable achievement—at Chartres, Reims, Bourges, Amiens, Laon, and Rouen; at Sens, Strasbourg, Noyon, Meaux, and other sites where great webs of masonry and colored glass still thrust their towers toward the skies, lasting memorials to the centuries of faith and enterprise. When the Romanesque church at Chartres burned

The first of the truly Gothic cathedrals, Notre Dame on the Île de la Cité, remains an enduring symbol of medieval Christendom.

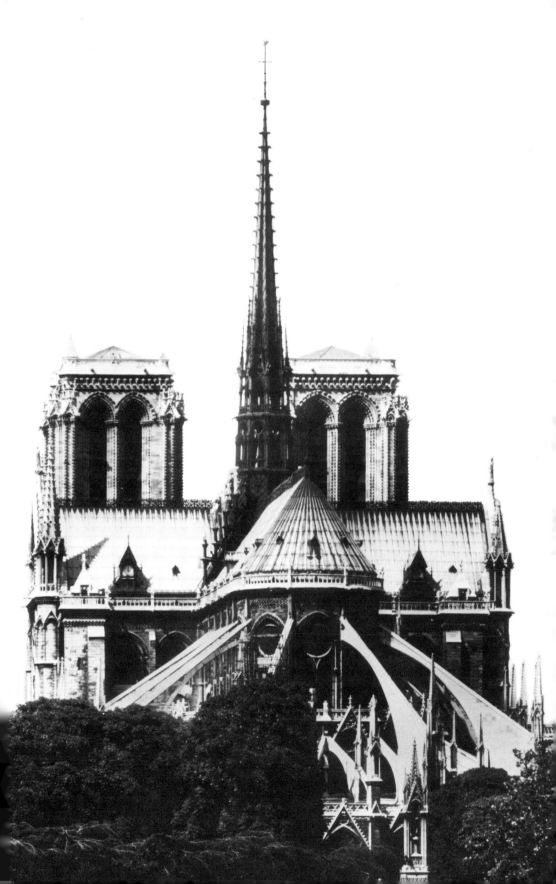

in 1194 it was decided to rebuild it—in the Gothic style—with the confident expectation that its principal relic, the Virgin's tunic salvaged from the fire, would attract enough pilgrims bearing gifts to cover the expense. And so it happened. The "new" Chartres that rose from the ashes became one of the most celebrated of all Gothic structures.

Associated from the start with some of these cathedrals, there developed during the same centuries centers of learning that flowered into great universities where the intellectual life of the Middle Ages was given its ultimate form. Here again Paris played a dominant role. The cathedral school of Notre Dame became a prototype of the universities that spread about northern Europe. It was at the University of Paris that Peter Abelard studied and taught in the twelfth century, where the critical issues he raised earned him the wrath of Saint Bernard of Clairvaux—from which he had to flee for refuge at the monastery of Cluny, and where he had met, tutored, and loved Héloïse with such tragic consequences. To the University of Paris also came the Italian Saint Thomas Aquinas to study with the famed German scholar Albertus Magnus in preparation for the compilation of his great *Summa theologica.* This work was nothing less than a summation of all the knowledge available at the time, compiled and designed to support the Christian faith against all doubts and controversy. It was one of the supreme achievements of the Middle Ages.

Paris was becoming a "city of teachers—the first city of teachers the medieval world had known," and to its proliferating colleges in the Latin Quarter came students from all Christendom. In 1200, as a result of a riot between the students and the king's troops, in which some of the former were killed, Philip Augustus, condemning his own royal official who had put down the trouble, granted the students immunities that would discourage them from going elsewhere for their education. The Sorbonne, the first endowed college of the university, was founded about 1257 by Robert de Sorbon, chaplain and confessor of Louis IX. (Over years to come its fame grew prodigiously, until its name alone was sometimes used to designate the University of Paris.) In the thirteenth century there were as many as twenty thousand foreign students resident in the city. Paris was not only the capital of France; it was the capital of knowledge in the Western world.

Although Latin was the language of the universities, the French

A fashionable fifteenth-century duchess with her attendants

tongue had won wide currency since the grandsons of Charlemagne first gave it official recognition in their treaty of 842. French crusaders and the French traders who followed them helped spread their vernacular throughout the Mediterranean world. French was becoming Europe's *lingua franca*. As Dante's master pointed out, French was spoken in the Holy Land, in Sicily, in Naples (which the Normans had conquered), and at the English court. Marco Polo wrote in French, and in 1206 Saint Francis of Assisi (named Francesco, or Frenchman, because his Italian father, Pietro Bernardone, was on a business trip in France when he was born) went off into the woods joyously singing a French song to herald the kingdom of Christ. By the twelfth century the *chansons de geste,* epic poems telling of high and mighty deeds and the earliest examples of French vernacular literature, were being sung to musical accompaniment before audiences throughout the land—at the courts of nobles and as inspirational entertainment along the pilgrimage routes at shrines where heroes of the past were said to be buried. Although they were accepted by medieval listeners as true history, they were in fact dramatic legends. Oldest and most famous of them all, the *Chanson de Roland* gives an imaginary account of an episode in Charlemagne's retreat from Spain more than three centuries earlier. At Hastings in 1066, it is said, the Norman *jongleur* Taillefer sang of Roland as he advanced with the army of William the Conqueror. In the later Middle Ages, Henry Adams wrote, this story "was chanted by every minstrel—known by heart, from beginning to end, by every man, woman, and child, lay or clerical—translated into every tongue—more intensely felt . . . in Italy and Spain than in Normandy and England. . . ."

With the dawn of the fourteenth century the prestige and the destiny of France seemed secure. At least two of the later Capetians, Louis IX and his grandson Philip IV, were memorable monarchs in an illustrious line. Louis' scrupulous fairness and honesty in honoring his feudal obligations and his treaties was an anachronism in an age when guile and power were better suited to advance the cause of the French monarchy. His crusading adventures were a sorry failure and he died a martyr's death in distant Africa. But he was remembered best for his virtues. In 1297 he was canonized, and as Saint Louis he remains a revered legend with no peer but Joan of Arc as an enduring and exalted symbol of France's national spirit.

Philip IV, called Philip the Fair because he was handsome, was more seriously concerned with strengthening the monarchy at any cost, and this he succeeded in doing by every means that came within his control, or within the control of the bureaucracy that managed his government for him. When he levied taxes on the French clergy of one half their annual income to finance his extended royal administration, he came into direct conflict with the papacy—a confrontation from which Philip emerged triumphant. In the course of that disagreement his agents actually assaulted the pope in his summer residence, a humiliation which seems to have hastened the death of the Holy Father. Shortly thereafter, a French archbishop was enthroned as Pope Clement V, a pope who never reached Rome but who rather established his permanent residence at Avignon in the south of France. There, a few years later, was built the enormous and splendid fortified structure known as the Pope's Palace that still rises majestically over the Rhone River and above the red-tiled roofs of the city's houses. Some of its towers are over 160 feet high; the enormous mass of the building covers about seventy thousand square feet.

The papal seat, filled by a succession of Frenchmen, remained there from 1309 to 1377, a span of time so close to the seventy-year captivity of the Jews in Babylon that the period has been called the Babylonian Captivity of the papacy. This episode signaled the descent of the papacy from the heights of influence and authority it had commanded for centuries past—a descent hastened by the pope's fiscal practices that seemed to many, clerics as well as laymen, to border on extortion. Petrarch, a good Catholic who had opportunities to witness such dealings during a stay at the court of Avignon, referred to the papacy as the Whore of Babylon.

After the pope had finally returned to Rome in 1378, an election took place in which the cardinals chose two popes; first, under pressure from Roman mobs, an Italian, then, upon reconsideration, a Frenchman. The former remained in Rome; the latter retreated to Avignon. This Great Schism, as it is called, within the Church lasted until 1417. At times there were even three rival popes, each hurling anathemas at the other two. The rupture quite naturally reduced the temporal (as well as the spiritual) authority of the Holy Father—authority which would be assumed by the separate monarchs of Europe within their

own national spheres. The diminishing role of the papacy was one of many changes that marked the waning of the Middle Ages.

But meanwhile, for more than a century, France knew troubled times. In 1328 the Capetians finally ran out of direct male heirs. Abiding by what has been called the Salic law, which forbade the succession through a female of the line, the peers of the realm chose as king Philip VI of Valois, nephew of Philip the Fair. With this development, Edward III of England, grandson of Philip the Fair, nephew of the last Capetian ruler, and son of their sister Isabel—uncontestably a French prince—laid counterclaim to the throne of France, a claim he asserted by force of arms. The Hundred Years' War had started.

From start to finish and on through a bloody aftermath this was a feudal and a dynastic struggle—one that had its inception when the Norman Conquest gave a strong French faction based on both sides of the Channel. When the war actually began in 1327 the only French territory held by the English king, as vassal to the king of France, was the southwestern duchy of Aquitaine or Guyenne. (From this region, with Bordeaux as its capital, came the clarets of which the English have been so fond for so many centuries with such good reason.) At the war's end in 1458, the English had been ousted altogether and forever

A contemporary depiction of the dance of death

from French soil, except for Calais which was taken some years later. But there were points between times when it seemed quite probable that the Frenchmen from England, with allied countrymen from the mainland, might master the whole country.

As the world changed about them, the French war lords had lingered in the age of chivalry. At Crécy in 1346 the English "churls" with their longbows mowed down the flower of French knighthood in a defeat *moulte grande et moulte horrible*. A year later, during the siege of Calais, Philip of Valois politely asked his English foe to come out from an impregnable position so that they might agree on some field of battle where the game of war could be played with proper courtesy. Disheartened by his adversary's refusal to follow the rules, Philip broke camp without fighting at all, and in a few months Calais fell to the English. But the lesson had to be learned all over again, first at Poitiers in 1356, then at Agincourt in 1415 where, encased in their heavy armor, the incurable French nobles all but sank in the mire under a shower of arrows from still other English archers.

When the hapless Charles VII became the king of France in 1422 the war was in its eighth grim decade and the kingdom he claimed as his rightful inheritance was at the lowest ebb of its fortunes. This tenth child of a madman, Charles VI, who had actually disinherited his son in favor of an English relative, and of a mother of loose morals who disowned him (it was widely reported that he was a bastard—no matter of shame at the time, but a shadow on his claim to the throne), this ill-omened youth was beleaguered in the small city of Bourges, south of Paris. His enemies contemptuously dubbed him the king of Bourges. An English king then reigned in Paris; English forces occupied all the land from the Channel to the Loire, as well as the fair duchy of Aquitaine. The powerful and autonomous duke of Burgundy, whose court at Dijon was the most brilliant in the land, tolerated the invaders and even abetted them. Brittany, ever mindful of its own independent traditions, wavered between allegiances.

Charles' military leaders were themselves independent contractors who between battles with the enemy roamed the land with their mercenaries, raping, stealing, burning, and killing. The years revolved in a murderous cycle of war and brigandage, of pestilence and famine. In one of those years, at least, no harvest reached Paris. By day and by night wolves drifted in from the ravaged countryside to scratch for freshly buried cadavers or to carry off living infants. Those were days of despair symbolized by pictures of the dance of death (*danse macabre*) that were painted on the walls of churches and cemeteries. In other paintings Christ, earlier depicted as a triumphant figure, came to be shown as the man of sorrows and of death, naked, bleeding, and crowned with thorns. Like Christ, as it has been said, France knew all the bitterness and weakness of a Passion. It was during those years that the poet François Villon grew up, and out of his turbulent youthful experience wrote with deep sadness of his own obsessive visions of death and decay. The optimism of the preceding century, when men were busy building the City of God, had dissolved in doubt and despair. In one haunting sentence Villon wrote his epitaph for the Middle Ages: "But where are the snows of yesteryear?" In those circumstances, trade and commerce came to a standstill. France was close to ruin.

In the winter of 1428–29 the English laid siege to Orléans, the principal city in Charles' rump of a kingdom, about midway between Paris and Bourges. Had Orléans fallen, there would have been pitifully little left of that kingdom. Then, as if in direct response to a widely whispered prophecy that an armed virgin would drive the English from the land, Joan of Arc appeared, raised the siege of Orléans, and persuaded the hesitant king to be crowned and anointed at Reims, where Clovis had been baptized. By that ritual the stain of bastardy was automatically removed; Charles was the true king of France. Eight years later he won Paris back from his English relatives. By then Joan had been captured by Burgundians, sold to the English, and convicted of witchcraft and heresy, burned at the stake in the old market place of Rouen, in still hostile Normandy, without a gesture from the king to aid or comfort her.

In 1444 Charles arranged a truce with the English, which gave him an opportunity to organize, for the first time, a permanent standing army—an army not only of cavalry, but of archers and crossbowmen—and, most importantly, the largest artillery of cannon, mortars, and other weapons "that ever the memory of men had seen in the possession of a Christian king." That, in turn, had been made possible by new powers of taxation that had been granted to the king by the Estates General (representatives of the clergy, nobles, and commons) as a measure, painful but necessary, to help him meet the emergencies of the war. Meanwhile, the duke of Burgundy had switched sides in return for a confirmation of his autonomy from Charles. In 1453 the English—the "Goddams" as they were called—were finally driven out of France. Now it was their turn to have a madman for a king, in the person of Henry VI.

But the French king's position was not yet secure. It was still threatened by fractious and scheming lords of the land, separately and in coalitions, who sought to maintain and aggrandize their feudal privileges and authorities—most seriously threatened by those dukes of Burgundy who had earlier betrayed the anointed sovereign, then compromised with him, and now sought to reconstitute that bothersome middle kingdom that had so long before, in 843, been formed by the treaty that divided Charlemagne's empire among his three grandsons. More blood was shed, but by craft and guile, by patience and persistence, by luck and struggle, the son of Charles VII, Louis XI, overcame the last of those feudal lords. When, in turn, his son, Charles VIII, married the heiress to the duchy of Brittany in 1491 most of the land that is France today had been won back or acquired by other means, and incorporated in the royal domain.

CHAPTER IV

FRENCH
RENAISSANCE

fter elaborate negotiations, in June, 1520, Francis I and Henry VIII, the kings of France and England, held a meeting of extraordinary pomp and circumstance on the Field of the Cloth of Gold just outside Calais. "Those sons of glory, those two lights of men," as Shakespeare wrote of them in describing the occasion, were both still in their twenties; both were outstanding examples of the "new monarchs" of the time, undisputed rulers of sovereign and major national states that had emerged from the feudal past; and both were out to make a smashing impression before a host of witnesses.

The celebrated encounter took its name from the cloth of gold that covered the pavilion where the two kings met. A gigantic temporary "palace," sumptuously decorated and furnished with a profusion of golden ornaments, was erected for the reception of Henry, and some 2,800 tents were put up in nearby fields to accommodate lesser dignitaries. There were jousting and wrestling matches in which both monarchs participated; mountebanks entertained the royal retinues; mendicants and vendors mingled with ladies in gorgeous attire and knights of the realm no less splendidly garbed in their own fashion; and enor-

Diane de Poitiers in the guise of Diana the huntress, by the French Renaissance sculptor Jean Goujon

mous quantities of food and drink were consumed. All in all it was a pageant of unprecedented magnificence—and of little or no practical consequence. By such a flattering and elaborate reception on French soil (Calais itself was still held by England) Francis had hoped to win Henry as an ally in a struggle to contain and defeat the newly elected Holy Roman Emperor, Charles V; and in this he did not succeed.

The events leading up to that gala occasion can be briefly told. When, thirty years earlier, Charles VIII had all but completed the consolidation of France under his sovereign rule by marrying Anne of Brittany, that lady was betrothed to Maximilian of Austria, who also coveted her duchy and who was then the (uncrowned) Holy Roman Emperor. Charles had, as well, inherited from his father a claim to the kingdom of Naples, and in 1494 he set out for Italy to assert his rights. He had fanciful visions of going on to retake Constantinople from the Turks and being crowned emperor of the East, and he actually entered Naples with the crown of the defunct Eastern Empire on his head. However, in a few months he was forced to retreat to France where several years later, in 1498, he cracked his skull against a low lintel in his favorite chateau at Amboise in the Loire valley and died at the age of twenty-eight, his fragile dreams of empire unrealized.

Then, to clinch the French claim to Brittany, his cousin and successor, Louis XII, also married Anne, divorcing his first wife in order to do so. And Louis also led his armies into Italy on expeditions that were longer and more complicated but no more fruitful in the end than that of Charles, in spite of heroic efforts by that perfect knight *sans peur et sans reproche,* the chevalier Bayard, who at one point held a bridge singlehandedly against an opposing army.

The lure of Italy took many forms. Beyond all thought of empire there was the attraction of Tuscan cypresses, Roman ruins, Neapolitan sunshine, and the newly revealed marvels of Renaissance art and architecture. As he passed through Milan, Louis was so enchanted by Leonardo da Vinci's "The Last Supper" he had to be dissuaded by his courtiers from cutting it off the wall of Santa Maria delle Grazie and shipping it back to France. Following his own retreat from Italy, now a somewhat worn-out widower in his late middle years, he married Mary Tudor, sister of Henry VIII. (Like Anne, she too was already betrothed to an Austrian prince, young Charles, who within a few short years was to become Holy Roman Emperor and the lifelong rival of Francis I. Whenever it could be managed the Austrian royal house was content to "marry" territory rather than fight for it.) Mary was an energetic, eighteen-year-old beauty, and to please his young bride Louis went to dances and kept late hours—but this he would sustain for only a brief time. In January, 1515, two months after the wedding, he died and his crown passed on to Francis I.

In the very first year of his reign Francis also succumbed to the blandishments of martial glory in the south, and like his two predecessors he charged across the mountains into Italy. Intoxicated by his early successes there, he too dreamed of bringing East and West together once more under a single crown. He also had visions of becoming Holy Roman Emperor and, against the advice of his counsellors, prepared his candidacy for that most prestigious office. However, in 1519, upon the death of Maximilian, the electors chose Charles of Austria to wear the imperial honors. As Emperor Charles V this young incumbent claimed dominions of vast extent and enormous wealth—a greater empire than Europe had known since the time of Charlemagne, almost eight centuries earlier. As ruler of Spain and Austria, the Netherlands, and important parts of Germany, Italy, and Burgundy, he controlled territories that threatened the very existence of France from every side.

It was under such circumstances and against those odds that Francis staged the elaborate performances on the Field of the Cloth of Gold. At those ceremonies he won a wrestling match with Henry, and that may have been a diplomatic blunder. In any case, with Cardinal Wolsey as adviser, Henry immediately thereafter chose to support the emperor in the international struggle. Francis turned where he could for allies against the coalition ranged against him—to Scotland, Scandinavia, Germany, and even to the Turks under Suleiman the Magnificent. The last—the most anti-Christian head of Moslem's greatest power—made a strange bedfellow for His Most Christian Majesty, the king of France. On the other hand, it was the armies of Charles, His Catholic Majesty of Spain as well as Holy Roman Emperor, that sacked the Eternal City at one point in the long, dreary contest; raping nuns, slaughtering hospital patients, kindling fires with precious manuscripts, and stabling horses in sacred shrines. These were obviously anything but crusades. In the end both sides gave up the struggle to

attend to urgent internal problems. France lost its claims in Italy, and the emperor won no lasting hold on French territory.

However, if Francis was unable to make Italy French, he had more success in making France Italian; that is to say, in awakening his own land to the large new visions that had been liberated with the Italian Renaissance. By the most lavish patronage he tempted to his court the greatest talents of the time. "I will choke you with gold," he promised Benvenuto Cellini to entice him to France; and that extravagant liar, professional philanderer, and remarkable genius did in fact come to serve for a while as an artist in residence, so to speak, at Paris and at Fontainebleau. Other masters of great renown answered the royal summons, Primaticcio and that "faultless painter" Andrea del Sarto among the rest. The aged Leonardo da Vinci also came north at Francis' urging (he was promised seven thousand pieces of gold and "a palace

An anonymous artist's version of the Field of the Cloth of Gold shows Henry VIII (at left) riding out of Calais to meet Francis I.

of his own choice in the most beautiful region of France"), only to die shortly after his arrival—as legend has it, in the arms of the king at the chateau of Amboise, where Charles VIII had died. Upon the artist's death, two of his paintings, the "Mona Lisa" and the "Virgin and Child and Saint Anne," now among the most celebrated treasures of the Louvre Museum, went to Francis. (Louis XII had already acquired Leonardo's "Madonna of the Rocks," now also in the Louvre.) Even Michelangelo accepted the king's invitation to visit France, but in the end found himself too absorbed by his work in Rome to leave it. Raphael, too, found it impossible to accept repeated flattering proposals by Francis, although seven of his paintings found their way to the Louvre as a legacy of the monarch.

A decade or so after his coronation, Francis announced his intention "to reside in our good city of Paris . . . being aware that our castle of the Louvre is the most convenient and appropriate place for us to dwell; and for this reason we have decided to repair and put it in order." The old tower that had stood for three centuries was torn down in four months. One contemporary citizen noted in his journal that it was a great pity since the tower was "very beautiful, high, and strong, and well suited to imprison men of great renown." But then little more was done for the next twenty years, although in 1546 Francis had the old structure lavishly decorated to receive Charles when the emperor made an extraordinary military expedition across his royal enemy's country, during a lull in their conflicts, in order to quell a rebellion among his subjects in the north.

Meanwhile, in the valley of the Loire River, great chateaux—Chambord, Blois, Azey-le-Rideau, Amboise, and others—were rising or being transformed under the influence of Italian designers and architects into French versions of the Renaissance style. These were sumptuous constructions, pleasure palaces rather than feudal keeps. They were not so much permanent residences as way stops in the pursuit of courtly diversions. And in good part, fortunately, they remain to delight today's traveler down the length of that pleasant valley, so fairly termed the garden of France. Nearer to Paris, Francis built the magnificent, huge palace that still stands in its forest setting at Fontainebleau, and Saint-Germain-en-Laye on its bluff commanding the winding turns of the Seine just west of the city. There, eight months before his death in 1547, remembering his promise to "put the Louvre in order" and make it a suitable royal headquarters, he set in train a series of building operations that in time—over three more centuries— would make that palace among the most impressive structures in all Europe, as it still is while it serves as a museum and for offices of a republican government.

Francis' court, wherever he held it, comprised the most brilliant gathering of lords and ladies that Europe had yet seen; a court which in its splendor foretold the extravagant displays at Versailles under Louis XIV more than a century later. The king, handsome philanderer that he was, fully appreciated a current epigram that compared a court without ladies to a "garden without flowers," and ladies dominated his courtly circles. The king's sister, Margaret of Navarre, was a writer and an intellectual who corresponded with Erasmus and patronized

Francis I in his court, a center of Renaissance learning, listening to a scholar
OVERLEAF: *Chambord, Francis' palatial Loire valley hunting lodge*

Rabelais, two of the most illustrious minds of the time. Francis sent to Florence for fourteen-year-old Catherine de Médicis as a wife for his son, Henry, and she brought with her the taste of the Medicis' and some of their money to indulge it (although Henry's mistress, Diane de Poitiers, an older woman, held a dominating influence over him during most of his adult life). Mary Queen of Scots, wife of Francis' grandson, persuaded Pierre de Ronsard to publish his odes, which made that author so famous that Paris students fought just to touch his robes as he walked by.

Ronsard, with Joachim du Bellay, led a small group of writers, known as *La Pléiade,* whose professed purpose was to strengthen and enrich the French vernacular and to develop a French literature that would challenge the triumphs of antiquity. Such efforts reflected a new, strong, and growing nationalist sentiment, a sentiment that quite naturally focused on the prestige and the prowess of the monarch, now so firmly established. The king ruled by his own will and pleasure. Deprived of their feudal props and privileges, ill-equipped and disinclined to find gainful occupation, the members of the nobility turned to the king for favors and handouts; they became courtiers and retainers, in effect parasites that fed on the royal institution. Justice became relatively uniform throughout the kingdom, meted out by the king's judges; and the king's language (derived from the old *langue d'oil* of the Île-de-France and other northern provinces) replaced Latin as the official language of the courts of the land—of the *nation,* as it might now be called.

The average Frenchman suffered little enough from the Italian campaigns of the Valois kings. On the contrary, following the miseries visited on France during the Hundred Years' War, these were years of economic recovery and progress. The population increased; during Francis' reign it was more than twice as large as Spain's, five times that of England. Paris was the largest city of western Europe. The prodigality of the court alone called for ever-increasing production. Through trade and privateering some share of the treasure from the New World reached France, increasing the supply of money, stimulating new enterprise, and leading to a rise in prices. New crops—melons, artichokes, asparagus—were introduced from Italy, along with the silkworm and Italians who taught France the secret of transforming the silken fibers produced by those larvae into textiles of sheer beauty.

It was the citizens of Lyons, where the silk industry had already become an enterprise of great importance, who, in 1524, financed the voyage of the Florentine Giovanni da Verrazano, in the course of which he claimed Newfoundland for France and, first of Europeans, explored the spacious bay that would one day, as New York was formed, become the major gateway to the New World. A few years later Jacques Cartier of Saint-Mâlo in Brittany also sailed westward, entered the Saint Lawrence River, and returned with a number of red-skinned natives who spoke of their "Canada" (that was the name of a Huron Indian village which Cartier supposed to be close to Tartary). In 1517, shortly after his coronation, Francis had founded the future Le Havre at the mouth of the Seine in Normandy, an outlet on the western ocean, to become the most important Atlantic port in France.

Meanwhile, throughout the forty years of his reign, Francis continued his vainglorious warfare with the Hapsburgs. When that contest was finally ended by treaty in 1559 the king and the emperor were both dead. Wearied beyond endurance by the heavy weight of his imperial scepter, Charles had sought peace for his soul in a monk's cell. From that ultimate retreat he divided his vast holdings between his brother Ferdinand and his son Philip. As his share, Ferdinand received Austria and the imperial title; Philip acquired Spain with its New World dependencies and, among other territories, the Netherlands.

By then Francis had already been succeeded by his son who took the French crown as Henry II in 1546. This new young monarch was passionately fond of hunting and jousting, a proclivity that cost him his life. On July 1, 1559, in the course of a tournament staged to celebrate the long-awaited peace (and the diplomatic marriage of his daughter to Philip of Spain), Henry suffered a rare accident in a jousting match. A sliver from a shattered lance pierced his eye and reached his brain. Within days he was dead.

That was a turning point in the history of France. A tiny sliver of wood accomplished in a very short time what the imperial armies had been unable to do for the forty years past; it destroyed the Valois monarchy and reduced France to impotence in the rivalry of nations. For the next forty years France was again ravaged by internal disturbances that threatened to tear the country asunder.

All Western Christendom was in turmoil during most of the sixteenth century and well into the seventeenth, quite apart from the contest between the Valois' and the Hapsburgs. Profound disagreements
about matters of dogma and ecclesiastical practices had split the
Church itself into warring factions. Calls for reforms within the
Church were almost as old as Christianity, but now they reached a
clamor that led to the greatest religious upheaval since the message of
Christ had conquered the Roman Empire so many centuries earlier.
That upheaval, the Reformation as we call it, was felt far beyond the
confines of religious controversy; it not only involved changes in the
civil and social order of large areas of Europe, but led to new patterns
of international strategy and rivalry.

In the end, most of the northern countries—England, Germany, the
Low Countries, Scandinavia, and Switzerland—broke away from the
Roman confession, violently when violence was necessary to the purpose. The Mediterranean world remained faithful to the Holy See. In
France for various reasons that large issue was deferred until a relatively late date. When it was finally joined, shortly after the death of
Henry II in 1559, it precipitated a series of frightful civil wars that in
character were as much political and dynastic as religious. They ended
only at the close of the century when further bloodshed and butchery,
ostensibly in the name of divine justice, became too sickening to face.
Better a "peace without God" than a "war for Him" at such a staggering cost in human life and misery.

One major reason for other countries to break with Rome grew from
the desires of their kings and princes to stem the flow of money out of
the parishes of their lands and into the coffers of the pope; to seize the
very substantial material possessions of the Church within their dominions; and to assume more direct moral control over their own subjects. In short it was an effort, only marginally concerned with religious
issues, to assert their national independence. A year after his coronation, in 1516, Francis I had already accomplished this aspect of the
"reformation" by signing a peaceable agreement with the pope, which
in effect brought the resources of the Church in France into the king's
hands. There was no need thereafter to part from Rome on that score.
As one reporter observed, Francis had thereby assumed the disposition
of "ten archbishops, eighty-two bishoprics, five hundred and twenty-

seven abbeys, [and] an infinitude of priories and canonries"—a prerogative that won him the "utmost servitude and obedience" of prel-
ates and laymen alike who sought benefices of one sort or another.

Even that diplomatic coup did not provide revenue enough to meet
Francis' increasing war debts; and it did not quiet those who called for
other reforms. Some years before Luther nailed his ninety-five theses
upon the door of the Court Church at Wittenberg in 1517, the essen-
tials of Lutheranism were being taught in Paris and were winning adherents, including the king's sister Margaret. At almost precisely the
same time, John Calvin was born in the cathedral town of Noyon in
Picardy. And by the time he reached maturity, there was a French
Protestant party, very soon to develop into a church in its own right
with Calvin, exiled in Geneva for his heresies, as its guiding light.

The French Calvinists, or Huguenots as they were called, held their
first ecclesiastical council in 1559, the year Henry II made his peace
with the Hapsburgs, and the year he died of his jousting accident. Almost from the moment of his accession to the throne twelve years
earlier, Henry had taken severe action against the heretics within his
Catholic realm. Ghastly punishments had been visited upon those who,
when accused, would not recant; they were burned alive or their
tongues were cut out. Mere suspects were cast into dungeons from
which many never emerged alive. It was small wonder that Calvin
hailed the king's death as a merciful dispensation of Providence. But
even after his death, Amboise, where his young son and successor was
in residence, was surrounded by a forest of gallows, and from the chateau windows the new monarch could see severed heads stuck on pikes.
But like the early Christians, the Huguenots drew strength from persecution. And increasingly they won adherents in high places.

Three young sons of the dead king by Catherine de Médicis came to
the throne in fairly rapid succession, none of them capable of contain-
ing the turbulent, divisive forces that rocked the country—even with
the practiced intrigue of their mother to help them. ("God has left me
with three small children," she wrote her daughter, the queen of Spain,
"and a wholly divided kingdom.") The eldest boy, who took the
crown as Francis II, died within two years of his ascendancy at the age
of nineteen. Next came Charles IX who mounted the throne as a minor
and died at the age of twenty-four in 1574. Then the youngest of the

three unfortunate brothers succeeded to the monarchy as Henry III, although he had small enthusiasm for that royal calling and won meager respect from his subjects. His delight in parading in woman's clothing with his *mignons,* or youthful male attendants, was but one of the peculiarities which strained the allegiance—and the credulity—of his people. "I shall never forget," the duke of Sully recalled years later, "the fantastic and extravagant equipage and attitude in which I found this prince in his cabinet: he had a sword at his side, a Spanish hood hung down upon his shoulders, a little cap, such as collegians wear, upon his head, and a basket full of little dogs hung to a broad ribbon about his neck."

During the reign of Charles IX a new herb, known as the "Queen's herb," or tobacco, was introduced to France from overseas and presented to Catherine de Médicis as a sovereign cure for ulcers, wounds, and comparable afflictions. But France was bleeding from ailments that wanted stronger remedies, and a stronger hand to apply them than the withering line of Valois kings could command. As the last three of that line eked out the years of their reigns, others came forward to contest the rule of the kingdom and challenge the succession to the throne. Each of these found in his religious affiliation support for his claim. Faith, politics, and pedigrees became inextricably mixed in the bloody civil wars France endured until the issue was settled—wars that resembled feudal brawls as great lords took to the field with their private armies, and lesser folk looked to them rather than to the king for protection.

The duke of Guise, a militant Catholic who had finally recaptured Calais from the English and who proudly traced his ancestry to Charlemagne, was for a time the uncrowned king of the land. He was killed in a battle with Protestant forces at Orléans in 1563, but he had a son and supporters to press his claims. Anne de Montmorency, constable of France, a rugged warrior who had fought with Francis I and who commanded his own substantial army, was a rival Catholic claimant; he, too, was killed—at the siege of Paris in 1567. And the Huguenots found their own titled contender for the throne in Henry of Bourbon, king of Navarre, who became in fact the legally acknowledged heir of the Valois'.

To chronicle the sordid, violent, and complex series of events by

While Catherine de Médicis acted as the real power behind their respective thrones, her sons, Francis II (above left), Charles IX (above), and Henry III (left), brought the Valois line to its ignominious close.

which this Henry became the first Bourbon king of France would be to tell of plots and murders, massacres and pitched battles, rapes and slaughter, in all of which little Christian charity or mercy was shown by Catholic or Protestant. At one point Protestants took a Catholic monastery and forced the monks to hang one another; at Orléans Catholic mobs burned a prisonful of Huguenot captives. The soil of France was soaked in French blood. Even the worst days of the Hundred Years' War had not seen such carnage and despoliation. Protestants mutilated statues that adorned the cathedrals at Bourges, Nîmes, Tours, and elsewhere; Catholics ruined Protestant places of worship.

Both factions sought foreign aid for their cause; the Protestants looked to England, Germany, and the Low Countries, the Catholics to Spain. Nothing the Valois kings or their scheming mothers tried could pacify and unify the realm.

Catherine made her most tragic blunder in attempting to arrange a détente between the rival factions in 1572. To reach some reconciliation she offered to marry her daughter, Margaret of Valois, to Henry of Navarre. At the last moment, fearful of the growing influence of the Huguenots, she reversed herself. On the morning of August 24, the day of the feast of Saint Bartholomew and immediately after the wedding, she gave way to panic and persuaded her son Charles IX to order a wholesale massacre of the principal Huguenots who had come to Paris to attend the ceremonies. Almost demented by uncertainties, the young king had reluctantly acceded to his mother's plan. "Well then, kill them all," he proclaimed, "that not a single man be left to reproach me." The Seine ran red with blood, and in the weeks that followed the butchery of Protestants was continued in the provinces. Philip II of Spain, Catherine's son-in-law, sent her his hearty congratulations and had a *Te Deum* sung; the pope struck a medal to commemorate the auspicious occasion and ordered an annual *Te Deum,* which was in fact long celebrated. On the other hand, Queen Elizabeth dressed in full mourning to receive the French ambassador and declared that "the deed had been too bloody." Even Ivan the Terrible of Russia, not unaccustomed to gore and violence, protested the Saint Bartholomew's Day Massacre. And France was more divided than ever.

Within a very few years the Huguenots had regathered their forces. Frightened by the consequences of his mother's sanguinary exploits,

when he became king two years afterward Henry III disowned any
responsibility for them. To ease tensions he made concessions to the
Huguenots. The Catholics in turn, lacking positive help from the king,
formed a Holy League, which was heavily financed by Spain, to further
their claims. In 1585 the last and most bitter of the religious wars broke
out. It is called the War of the Three Henrys after the three principals
of that name who came to grips in a struggle for power—Henry of
Navarre, now brother-in-law of the king and under the laws of the
kingdom the rightful heir to the throne, Protestant though he was in a
predominantly Catholic country; Henry of Guise, son of the duke who
had been murdered in 1565, leader of the Catholics, and king of France
in all but name; and Henry of Valois, whose crown tottered in the
balance. In a rare show of daring that simpering monarch eliminated
Guise by having him assassinated. Then came the king's turn. He was
assassinated by a Dominican monk who believed he had been instructed
by God to remove the degenerate and wavering Valois from all contention. Only Henry of Navarre remained to assert his rights, which
the dying king had confirmed on his deathbed.

Although his Protestant forces were outnumbered, the Bourbon
soundly thrashed his Catholic opponents, French and Spanish alike, on
the battlefield. But without Paris there could be no final victory, and
Paris would not tolerate a Huguenot pretender. Under siege Parisians
ate dogs, rats, cats, and grass rather than be starved into submission;
bones of animals and even of human corpses were ground for flour.
Thousands actually died of starvation and fever, but Paris held out.
Finally on July 25, 1593, the surviving Henry, conceding that "Paris
is well worth a Mass," abjured his Protestant faith, converted to
Catholicism, was admitted to Paris, and took up the rule of a sadly
lacerated kingdom. Five years later, to avoid any further religious
strife, he issued the Edict of Nantes, granting liberty of conscience to
all, perpetually and irrevocably, "without being questioned, vexed, or
molested." That same year he signed a peace with Spain, confirming
the one that had been agreed to forty bloody years before. And once
again, yearning for a return to order at all costs, the French people
looked to their king—the first Bourbon ruler—for single and supreme
leadership. Experience had proved there was no satisfactory alternative
to a strong monarchy.

CHAPTER V

A SPLENDID
CENTURY

he most lasting consequence of the Edict of Nantes was, no doubt, that it gave time for the idea and the ideal of religious tolera-tion to take root. Neither Catholics nor Protestants were then ready to accept such radical tenets. But the settlement imposed by Henry IV was an immediate and practical arrangement that suspended the threat of more civil warfare, of seemingly endless bloodshed, and of continu-ous economic stagnation. Of all this, the whole nation, Catholics and Protestants alike, had had enough for a time, and they accepted the compromise. The edict was thus a radical act, for it implied that peace and order in the kingdom were more important than religious uniform-ity. Ironically, the single Frenchman who could not legally exercise his choice of religion was Henry himself. If he were to wear his crown and exercise his authority from a solid base in Paris he had to remain a Catholic, at least in all outward respects.

The reconstruction of France after the chaos of the preceding forty years took time, foresight, and political courage. To aid him in this formidable undertaking Henry chose Maximilien de Béthune, whom he made duke of Sully and who proved to be a brilliant collaborator,

A marble bust of Jean Baptiste Colbert, carved by Antoine Coysevox

even if the two men did not always agree. It was against the opinion of
Sully that Henry, at a heavy cost, bribed those lords of the land who
had created a new feudalism during the recent wars, rather than batter
them into submission to the reborn monarchy. It would cost ten times
more to fight them, he reminded his counselor, than to pay them off.
Once again, it was contrary to the advice of his minister that Henry lent
his support to the adventurous expedition of Samuel de Champlain to
the New World. Champlain had fought with the king's armies against
the remnants of the Holy League, and relying upon his reports, Henry
staked out France's large claim to Canada in the North American continent. As Henry well understood, Sully was a master of finance and by
his guidance the treasury was replenished in relatively short order.
Confident in this new prosperity, Henry endeared himself to the mass
of Frenchmen, so many of whom had known only hunger and depriva-
tion during their lifetime, by voicing his wish that "there should be a
chicken in every peasant's pot every Sunday."

A 1635 view from the Pont Neuf, looking west toward the Louvre

Sully was an engineer, to boot, and he promoted public works along with agriculture. Under his administration forests were protected and swamps were drained. He planned a new system of highways (lined with elms), bridges, and canals, and as his plans materialized, France came to have the first thoroughfare that had been known since the great days of Rome; its waterways were likewise unsurpassed in the world. Down to this day France owes much to Sully for the beauty of her roads, forests, and countryside.

At the important center of that system of communications, and at the cultural and political center of the realm, Paris assumed new aspects. Henry's reign saw the completion of the Pont Neuf, oldest, most celebrated, and most important of the city's bridges, that spans the Seine at the western end of the Île de la Cité, connecting that island with the Right and Left Banks. Before any street in Paris had such a convenience, the Pont Neuf had sidewalks for pedestrians; its ample roadway, constructed more than three and a half centuries ago, accommodates today's heavy automobile traffic with less strain than many of the more modern thoroughfares in the city. Just east of the roadway as it crosses the Île was constructed the delightful three-sided place Dauphine, one of the first royal plazas in Paris and named in honor of the future Louis XIII, then six years old. It is still a delightful place to saunter in the heart of Paris.

Henry also undertook the construction of another, magnificent royal square, the place Royale (since 1800 known as the place des Vosges) which became so celebrated as a center of elegant and fashionable activity that it was known simply as "La Place"—and which in recent years has reclaimed attention as a notable landmark in the development of Europe's most attractive capital. It was then, too, that the celebrated Grande Galerie was added to the Louvre; this extension, more than a quarter of a mile long and one hundred feet wide, paralleling the Seine, was the longest structure of its kind in the world, and with its priceless art treasures it is today a mecca for visitors from all over the world. (On the lower floors of that addition hundreds of artists and craftsmen lived and worked as guests of the king, a royal accommodation that was continued for two centuries—until Napoleon I revoked all such privileges.) Paris was becoming the Western world's classic example of urban development in the grand manner.

Quite aside from his gallantry on the battlefield and the grandeur of the public works that flourished with his approval, Henry IV was—and continues to be—one of the most popular kings of French history by the very nature of his personality. His kindness and his compassion, his humor and his ardor, remembered in an abundance of friendly anecdotes, brought him the affectionate regard of his people. Although he was twice married, first to Margaret of Valois, a marriage that was annulled after a number of childless years, then to Marie de Médicis, who produced his children regularly, he also had an all but endless succession of mistresses who provided him with a flourishing crop of bastards, a number of whom were acknowledged and ennobled. He was, as a popular rhyme put it, the *vert gallant*—a king who could not only drink and fight, but make love with the best of them—talents that did not diminish his reputation among his countrymen. However, like Henry of Guise and Henry of Valois before him, Henry IV met his fate at the hands of an assassin on May 14, 1610. Four years after his death a bronze equestrian statue was erected to his memory in the middle of the Pont Neuf. It was the first such effigy in France to be displayed on a public route. A copy of it now stands by the roadside across from the place Dauphine, overlooking what is called the square of the Vert Galant at the top of the Île de la Cité.

Henry had got the Bourbon dynasty off to a promising start; a start from which over the next two hundred years, during the reigns of four successive Louis'—Louis XIII, XIV, XV, and XVI—the dynasty would rise to heights of unprecedented grandeur, then descend to depths of impotence. The first of those four, a son of Henry IV, was but a child of nine when his father was murdered, and the parlement of Paris entrusted the regency to his mother, Marie de Médicis. Marie was a bloated, stupid, and obstinate woman—known in court circles as "the fat banker"—whom Henry IV had married to pay off a debt to her uncle, the grand duke of Tuscany. Soon all power was assumed by her unscrupulous Italian favorite, Concino Concini, husband of Marie's childhood companion. He became a marquis and marshal of France and a man widely disliked by the nobles of the country for the undeserved favors that were heaped upon him. Through his offices Italian representatives of the Catholic Church hoped to force the suppression of Protestantism in France. Sully, always a Huguenot, was obliged to quit his own office, and the financial reserves of the kingdom, which he had so closely guarded, were drained off into the pockets of avarice.

But the young king also bitterly resented Concini. In 1617, with Louis' connivance, the Italian was cut down as he was entering the Louvre; his wife was condemned to death and burned as a witch. At the age of sixteen Louis himself assumed power, removing his mother from his councils and, along with her, another of her favorites, Armand du Plessis, duke of Richelieu, the courtly young bishop of Luçon who had been elevated to the position of a secretary of state. Richelieu had earlier attached himself to Concini and as his protégé had hardly won the king's confidence or favor. "Here is a man," said the king, "who would greatly like to be in my council, but I cannot reconcile myself to it after all the things he has done against me." However, Richelieu's brilliance and his energy won wide recognition elsewhere. The pope went so far as to make him a cardinal in 1622; foreign ambassadors to the French court expressed surprise that a man of such outstanding

gifts should not be an important adviser to the king; and in April, 1624, Louis finally appointed Richelieu to his royal council. Four months later he became the chief minister of state.

The king's mother bitterly resented the growth of Richelieu's power; the king's wife strongly objected to Richelieu's policies; the king's silly and arrogant brother disliked Richelieu's interference with the privileges of the nobility; and the king himself was slow to put his complete trust in Richelieu. But the "secret great Cardinal," as a contemporary called Richelieu, finally and decisively shaped the destiny of France until his death in 1642. He was the first of a succession of strong ministers through whose efforts the French monarch became an absolute ruler and France itself became indisputably the supreme power in Europe.

At one point Richelieu described himself as "the most devoted subject and the most zealous servant that ever King had in this world." Others represented him as a sinister figure, ruthless, informed by his

Anne of Austria, Louis XIII, and Richelieu watch the world première of Mirame, *a play by Desmarets, at the cardinal's private palace theater.*

own secret service, protected by a personal bodyguard, and devious in his manipulation of the press—the prototype of a modern dictator. He was indeed both a statesman of rare vision and a political manipulator of exceptional cunning. He overlooked nothing and stopped at nothing to serve France by serving the king, with whatever means he could contrive to bring peace, prosperity, and power to the realm. His vision was large, his strategy was superb, and his talents were apparently inexhaustible. To reach his ends Richelieu followed three basic policies: to contain and humble the Hapsburgs, the ruling house of Austria whose head was traditionally the Holy Roman Emperor; to make the French nobility for once and all subservient to their monarch; and to do away with the special privileges, granted by Henry IV, that had made the Huguenots virtually a state within a state.

Before his death Richelieu had achieved those three goals. When he first rose to eminence in 1624, France was ringed around by the threat of Hapsburg power—from Spain, Austria, the Spanish Netherlands, northern Italy, and much of the Rhineland. It seemed as though the Hapsburgs might in fact dominate all western Europe and turn France into a dependency. In the absence of an adequate navy, the seaways out of France—the routes of maritime commerce—were plagued by piracy. Again grown independent, the French nobles did not hesitate to rise in revolt, and to call upon foreign aid to support their claims.

By 1642, when Richelieu died, through a combination of hidden diplomacy and open aggression he had secured the frontiers of France at every point on the compass. Spain and her allies had been turned back, France had assumed authority over the vital border region of Alsace, and held key fortresses on the Rhine and in the Alps and the Pyrenees. The military reputation of France was firmly established. At sea, the French navy, almost entirely Richelieu's creation, patrolled and controlled the coastal waters in war and in peace. The conspiracies of the nobles were repressed without pity. Richelieu pulled down the fortified castles of the most illustrious families of France; he even tried to prohibit dueling, that last stand of the feudal right of private warfare. The Huguenots were forced to relinquish their military and civil privileges, although they retained their freedom of worship, as pledged by Henry IV. With Sully's help, Henry had pacified France; with Richelieu's, Louis XIII reconstructed the kingdom.

Richelieu's statesmanship ranged far beyond the limits of power politics. He saw an incontestably strong government as the means to a higher end, a base for the creation of a French civilization that would be unmatched in grandeur, and he bent his protean talents toward that larger goal. He lent his encouragement to the development of all the arts of civilization. In 1635 he founded and became patron of the French Academy, an association of literary men whose mission was to improve the language and encourage the literature of France. To be counted among the "forty immortals" of the Academy (membership is limited to that number) remains to this day one of the most coveted distinctions in the world of letters. As chancellor of the Sorbonne, Richelieu procured for that venerable institution many of the privileges it was to enjoy over the years to come. He commissioned Jacques Lemercier, the most important of an illustrious family of architects, to reconstruct its decaying buildings, including the church where Richelieu was entombed upon his death; the only part of the reconstruction that remains intact today.

Richelieu did not, of course, call into being the authors, dramatists, artists, and other creative individuals who gave such distinction to this period, but he recognized and used their talents. Before his ministry had started, Mme de Rambouillet had already opened her salon—her famous Blue Room—to the best minds of Paris, whose meetings set an example that was widely imitated throughout France and in other lands. Richelieu himself was attracted to her circle, joining company with the great tragic dramatist and poet Pierre Corneille, with François de Malherbe, the court poet to Louis XIII who helped make Parisian French the standard language of the realm (and the international language of diplomacy), and with others of hardly less distinction, including a good number of the sharpest feminine intellects of the day, such as Mme de Sévigné and Mme de La Fayette. The fashion set by the success of the Rambouillet salon led to the excesses of refinement and preciosity in manners and social intercourse that Molière lampooned with brilliant satire in *Les Précieuses ridicules* and *Les Femmes savantes*. Nevertheless, the salon remained a significant factor in French culture for well over a century to come.

With Richelieu's personal encouragement the French theater was winning a reputation that would soon be unrivaled in Europe. In 1637

Corneille's *Le Cid* took Paris by storm—and aroused a bitter controversy over the classic canons of playmaking, which Corneille had
flouted. But he went on to other performances that won great acclaim,
and later in the century Racine and Molière added to the mounting
prestige of the French stage.

The cardinal would have liked to make Paris the artistic capital of
the Continent, and there were painters of outstanding merit working
in the city, such as the Flemish-born Philippe de Champaigne and the
Frenchman Simon Vouet. In the former's full-length portrait of Richelieu, his thin, erect body magnificently draped in his cardinal's robes,
his keen eyes riveted on the viewer, we have an imperishable and commanding image of this enigmatic man. Vouet spent fifteen years in
Rome, which was in fact the European center of artistic activity and of
patronage, before returning to Paris where he exercised a profound
influence on the development of the French school of painting.

But the greatest French painter of the day, Nicolas Poussin, preferred to live and work in Rome. Poussin was the first French artist to
win international fame, the only one to rank with Rembrandt, Rubens,
and Velázquez, and the classical perfection of the work he produced
in Rome set French art on a course that led it toward its greatest
achievements. The supremacy of French paintings in the centuries to
come—down to our own—goes back directly to Poussin. Two hundred
years later, when Cézanne said that he wanted to "do Poussin over
again after nature," he acknowledged Poussin's original powers of
organization that so impressed Poussin's own contemporaries.

There were other artists who contributed importantly to the growing prestige of French painting—Claude Gelée, renamed Lorrain
after his birthplace, who also worked in Rome and has been called the
"father of European landscape painting"; Georges de la Tour and the
brothers Le Nain whose realistically drawn, often humble subjects are
probably more admired today than when they were created; and among
still others, the engraver Jacques Callot who for political reasons ultimately refused any commissions from Richelieu.

In an entirely different sphere, in 1637, when Richelieu was at the
height of his eminence, René Descartes published a group of essays,
including his *Discourse on Method*, that was to have a profound influence on the direction of thought, science, and literature in years to

come. The starting point of his philosophy was his celebrated phrase *cogito, ergo sum,* "I think, therefore I am." Doubt itself cannot be doubted, because to doubt is to think, and to think is to exist in reality. Everything else is to be doubted until rational criticism proves its credibility. The full impact of that line of thought was felt a century later when the philosophers brought it to bear on problems of religious and political authority, with revolutionary consequences.

When Richelieu died in 1642, followed to the grave within six months by the king he had served so single-mindedly, the political scene in France changed almost overnight. Once again the heir to the throne, Louis XIV this time, was a small child; once again the queen mother, this time Anne of Austria, daughter of Philip II of Spain, was made regent; and once again, an Italian—a Sicilian—Giulio Mazarini, called Mazarin, became the principal minister of state. Actually, Mazarin had been recommended by Richelieu as his successor, and had been made a cardinal (although he had not been ordained a priest) on the recommendation of Louis XIII. Beloved of the queen, perhaps her secret spouse, this amazing adventurer ruled both Anne and France for the next eighteen years. Even after he came of age in 1652, Louis XIV did not attempt to suppress his cardinal-minister. In this the new king was wise. Mazarin was far more devious than Richelieu in his methods, but he pursued the same ends with the same tenacity, and when he died in 1661 he left Louis XIV a kingdom that was stronger than ever.

This had not been altogether easy. Mazarin inherited Richelieu's wars with the Hapsburgs, but those wars concluded in 1648 with the Treaties of Westphalia, which left the Holy Roman Empire virtually impotent. Those settlements completely vindicated Richelieu's policies; France emerged as the supreme arbiter of Europe. However, there were serious internal problems to contend with before the king could be complete master of his own realm. Almost at the same moment that France triumphed at Westphalia, barricades were thrown up in the streets of Paris in protest over the growing and arbitrary power of the king's government and the increasing fiscal burdens its policies had imposed on the populace—a protest first led by the parlement, then renewed by certain "Important Ones," as they were nicknamed—noble military leaders who thought they saw in the minority of the king and in the discontent of the people a good opportunity to express their own

Richelieu in his cardinal's robes, as depicted by Philippe de Champaigne

dislike of their Spanish queen and Italian minister and to contest the royal authority.

Those uprisings were derisively referred to as the *Fronde* (the French word for a sling), because stones were catapulted into Mazarin's windows by slingshot. But this was not child's play. It was more like a rehearsal of the French Revolution. The queen had to quit Paris with her young son and for a time Mazarin went into exile—without, however, losing his power over the regent. The disturbances lasted for five years. Had the opposition to Mazarin and the court been united it would have been a true revolution. But the enemies of the monarchy wore themselves out with their own contentious differences. Once again it became apparent that to most Frenchmen the commanding authority of the king, arbitrary and absolute as it might be, and engineered by a minister of dubious scruples, was preferable to the anarchical dispositions of the nobility. After a long series of contretemps, Louis XIV made a military entrance into Paris in October, 1652, at the age of fourteen, and the populace welcomed his return with relief. When Mazarin returned a few months later, he came "in triumph and all bedecked with glory." He had played a subtle game in outwitting and outwaiting his opponents. Those who had abused him most now stooped the lowest in acknowledging his mastery.

The *Frondeurs* were overcome, once again the nation was at peace with itself, and the king's supreme authority over his subjects was reaffirmed. But Mazarin still had vital work to do. The treaties signed at Westphalia in 1648 had not put a stop to the separate war between France and Spain (Spain had intervened in the affairs of the *Fronde*), which continued until 1659. By the terms of the peace treaty signed that year France added the northern province of Artois and some other areas to its territory.

However, in the end the most important point in that settlement was a marriage contract between Louis XIV and the infanta Maria Theresa, oldest daughter of Philip IV of Spain and potential heiress to the entire Spanish empire. It was stipulated in the contract that the infanta would forever renounce all claims to her inheritance, both for herself and for her descendants by Louis, upon payment of a very substantial dowry. That condition, Mazarin well knew, was beyond the resources of Spain to fulfill, a circumstance that would justify further French claims to

Spanish territory, and it did in fact become a dominating factor in European politics over another half century. Even America would be involved in the next century in the so-called War of the Spanish Succession, remembered in the New World as Queen Anne's War.

On June 9, 1660, Louis and Maria Theresa were married at Saint-Jean-de-Luz, a coastal town near the Pyrenees. Louis was not an enthusiastic bridegroom; he had another love. But he bowed to his royal obligation, and Mazarin, to avoid undesirable complications, cunningly persuaded him that his true love was faithless. That affair was ended. But Louis was only twenty-two; there was still time in his long life for many others.

Less than a year later, during the night of March 8, 1661, Mazarin died. When Louis awakened in the morning he was given this not unexpected news by the nurse who slept in the royal bedroom. Later that same morning he assembled the important Crown officials and informed them that thenceforth he himself would take over those functions of state which for so long had been administered by Mazarin, and before him by Richelieu. In the future the duties of ministers would be to advise, not to initiate. The king would not only reign, he would actually rule. The way toward that assumption of absolute authority had been well paved by both Richelieu and Mazarin, and Louis proved eminently capable of filling the role he assigned to himself. "The king's calling," he wrote, "is great, noble, and delightful when a man feels himself worthy to perform well everything he undertakes."

About his worthiness for this calling Louis suffered no doubts. He made himself the Grand Monarch, the Sun King of "terrifying majesty," and, in his own view, the divinely appointed instrument of God's will. He may never have said *L'État, c'est moi* ("The State, I am the State!"), but the phrase clearly expressed his concept of kingship. His personal will gave the most important and powerful state in Europe its direction and its sense of mission.

The *Fronde* had been the last general uprising of the nobility against the monarchy. The traditionally proud members of the aristocracy, whose resurgent insubordination had so often led France toward chaos, were now put to the royal service. Its leaders, deliberately shorn of both their power and the sources of their income, were bound to turn to the court to bask in reflection of the Sun King's glory, if they could, and to look for such rewards as the king ordained. Louis was a lavish sovereign, with a sublime disregard for the harsh realities of accounting and bookkeeping. As one of his financial advisers, with utmost deference, pleaded in a moment of desperation; "I entreat your Majesty to allow me to say that in war and in peace, Your Majesty has never consulted his finances to determine his expenditures. . . ."

On the other hand, Louis was quick enough to detect and condemn the extravagance of others, especially on the part of those who offered any semblance of competition with the royal dispensations. As a most important case in point, in August, 1661, only five months after Mazarin's death, the king was entertained at an extraordinary fete arranged by his superintendent of finance Nicolas Fouquet, at his magnificent chateau, Vaux le Vicomte, not far from Paris. Fouquet had been a favorite of Mazarin and had outdone the Italian in using his official position to amass a private fortune. He was immensely rich, he had good friends in high places, and he was popular among the wealthy. He hoped to succeed Mazarin as minister. The magnificence of the reception he provided for the king that August afternoon was all but unrivaled in French history. Fouquet's elaborate pleasure dome was built for him by Louis Le Vau, decorated by Charles Le Brun, and landscaped by André Le Nôtre, all of whom were the outstanding practitioners of their arts. Molière's *Les Fâcheux* was produced that night for the first time; the Italian-born composer Jean Baptiste Lully led the orchestra; the incomparable chef Vatel supervised the menu of a memorable banquet for some five hundred guests. There was an outdoor ballet, fireworks, and a final salute of cannons. The poet and fabulist Jean de La Fontaine was present and wrote that Heaven itself was jealous of the splendor of the occasion.

Louis was entertained—but he was not amused. At the king's table the service was of massive, solid gold, a particularly irritating indiscretion on the part of his host, for Louis had had to melt down his own golden equipment to meet the final expenses of state during the recent wars. Refusing to pass the night at Vaux, the king returned to Fontainebleau to nurse his indignation. Within three weeks Fouquet was arrested, tried, and imprisoned for life on a charge of embezzling public funds. And within a short time after that, Le Vau, Le Brun, and Le Nôtre, among others, were commissioned by the king to construct a

A detail of "Orpheus and Eurydice" painted by Nicolas Poussin, Louis XIII's official First Painter from 1640 to 1642

complex of buildings and gardens at Versailles that would far surpass Vaux and that would astonish the whole world with its grandeur.

That grandeur is indescribable, almost unbelievable. The cost was staggering. Louis himself was occasionally disconcerted by the figures (at one point he burnt his architect's accounts) and his subjects had reason to resent such enormous expenditures by the court. However, here was an inimitable declaration of the Sun King's eminence, such eminence as no European monarch had attained since the days of Rome's greatness. Many other kings and princes aspired to such a setting. "Little Versailles' " were built in their capitals by the envious rulers of other lands, but they were only pale, small reflections of the original.

Louis made Versailles his principal residence in 1682, happy to quit Paris and the Louvre where, as a youth, he had suffered indignities during the *Fronde*. And to Versailles swarmed the pick of the French aristocracy, by the thousands, each hopeful of some show of preferment by the king. Five thousand of them were accommodated at the palace; five thousand others, less fortunate, managed to find some sort of quarters in the adjacent village. Those who failed to contrive an appearance at the court were cut off from royal favors and benefices. It could be a ruinously expensive existence; Louis planned it that way. He forced magnificence on his courtiers, and he alone dispensed the largesse that made that possible. A mere rumor that the king had, in passing, made a casual remark to one of those dependents was enough to assure him of six months' credit with the village merchants.

In a brief history of France it may seem trivial to linger over the refinements of etiquette that were dictated at Versailles. Yet those details illuminate as nothing else can the nature of Louis' absolutism. A courtier who passed the royal dinner on its way to the king's table must bow as to the king himself, sweeping the floor with the plume of his hat while softly but audibly remarking that he had noted the passage of the royal meal. Who might sit down in the presence of whom, and under what circumstances, was at times a matter of delicate and prolonged negotiation—even an affair of state. Armchairs, chairs without arms, and stools represented three degrees of dignity which must be respected in any formal gathering, and negotiated in advance where there was any doubt about the precedences involved—all of which

issued from royal authority. There were those, of course, who must remain standing in the presence of others who were higher up in the hierarchy. From the moment he awakened to the time he went to bed Louis both commanded and was subjected to the most rigorous formalities. At the close of the day certain carefully chosen gentlemen of the court enjoyed the special and intimate privilege of attending the king as he sat on his toilet chair before retiring. (Louis took his own part in such ceremonies very seriously, and he assumed this posture regularly as a ritual whether or not he felt the need.)

To raise the money with which he could work his will and support his extravagances, for more than a score of years Louis depended upon Jean Baptiste Colbert, his minister for finance and economic affairs— a sort of universal manager of the domestic problems of the realm and

A bronze bust of Louis XIV, by the baroque sculptor Giovanni Bernini

Completed in 1688, Versailles, with its vast gardens, reflected the Sun King's passion for order and opulence.

one of the ablest administrators in French history. Colbert was the son of a clothier, a bourgeois, as most of Louis' chief servants were; he had no great affection for the nobility. He had managed Mazarin's infamous fortune, had been recommended by him to the king, and, following the Italian's death, had further won the king's favor by revealing to him some of Mazarin's hidden wealth. Like others in his position, he, too, lined his own pockets while doing the king's business; but that was in the nature of the business. Beyond that Colbert was a financial genius and he was dedicated to the glory of France under the rule of his sovereign.

His efforts to reform the fiscal affairs of France were ruthless and rigidly ordered. Thanks to the personal authority conferred upon him by the king, he severely punished officials guilty of malfeasance. (He helped to have Fouquet convicted for his frauds.) Some public loans were totally repudiated. False claims to tax exemptions were firmly resisted. Colbert rebuilt the navy and the merchant marine and fostered the growth of France's colonial interests. Everything possible was planned to make France economically self-sufficient. He reorganized and policed French industry so that it would be centrally controlled, like everything else in the kingdom, and so that uniform, high standards of production would be maintained—all to glorify the monarchy.

Colbert's firm authority extended over the arts, letters, and sciences. He founded the Academy of Science in 1666, and in 1671 the Academy of Architecture. He regimented Richelieu's French Academy, putting its members on a precise timetable for their scheduled meetings in the Louvre. Tardiness or absence was penalized; the king's clockmaker was responsible for keeping the exact time. He also reorganized the Academy of Paintings and Sculpture that Richelieu had established in 1648 (and that would control the character of French art for two centuries to come). He founded an academy at Rome, where French students of the arts were to be integrated into a system of royal tutelage and performance. Under his command, indeed, the practice of the arts became virtually a national industry and, in effect, a vast propaganda machine for Louis' regime. His first in command, the painter Charles Le Brun, was himself as much an institution as an artist—a rare artist who had a genius for organization.

In 1663 Le Brun was put in charge of the Gobelins manufactory, a

royal establishment that was commissioned to supply, in addition to its
celebrated tapestries, all the other furnishings and decoration required
or requested by the king for his various palaces. This included everything from hardware and bric-a-brac to the richest furniture and the
most elaborate mural paintings. Le Brun himself finished thirty paintings for the ceiling of the Galerie des Glaces at Versailles, among
other large projects. He was also in charge of fountains, fetes, and fireworks. Over all such matters he exercised the closest personal super-
vision. As it has often been said, Le Brun virtually created the Louis
XIV style, a style of almost overwhelming splendor and of a unity
unequaled in the history of art.

During the reign of Louis XIV France assumed the lead in all the
arts, thanks to royal patronage, the direction of the king's enlightened
ministers, and a rare conjunction of brilliant talents. Rarely in history
has any society produced such a galaxy of distinguished dramatists as
Molière, Racine, and Corneille; of such authors as La Rochefoucauld,
Bossuet, Boileau, and La Fontaine; of such artists and architects already mentioned; of such musicians as Lully, Couperin, and Charpen-
tier; and of such philosophers and scientists as Descartes and Pascal—
all of whom were at the height of their powers in this single reign.

Thanks to Colbert's indefatigable ministry France managed for
about twenty years to pay for the crushing luxury imposed upon it by
the Grand Monarch. Then, in 1683, Colbert died and his responsibilities were taken over by the marquis de Louvois, who had been and remained the king's immensely capable minister of war. From the start
of his career Louvois was determined to provide France—or Louis
XIV—with the largest, best armed and provisioned, and most disciplined and efficient army in the Western world, and in this he succeeded. (The word *martinet,* which we use today to describe a rigid
and demanding disciplinarian, comes from the name of the first inspec-
tor of the French infantry under Louvois, Jules Martinet.)

Before he was through France had a third of a million or more soldiers on the state payroll, a force enormously larger than the army that
had served the nation against the Hapsburgs one hundred years earlier
—and these were now soldiers of the king, and of no one else. Also
thanks to Colbert, France had for a while the largest and finest navy
in Europe. To complement this formidable war machine in securing

French domination over all other nations, Louis employed the most costly diplomatic measures to divide or buy off the enemies of his plans. "At one time," writes J. H. Herter, "he had on his payroll, the king of England, the king of Sweden, the Margrave of Brandenburg, and hosts of lesser German princes, a considerable part of the Dutch Estates General, the leaders of the king's government in the English Parliament, and the leaders of the opposition to that government."

For the last half century of his long reign, almost until his death in 1715, Louis was involved in intermittent warfare because of his determination to establish the undisputed hegemony of France over the entire European continent. The coalitions he contrived to help his cause, and the combinations that arose to counter it, formed, dissolved, and reformed in a bewildering complex of shifting alliances. There is little need to detail the succession of conflicts that ensued. At some time or another practically all the countries of Europe were involved in wars that ranged from the Mediterranean to the Baltic, fighting for or against Louis—mostly against—according to the chances they saw for their own salvation or betterment. At best it was a dreary and indecisive fracas in the course of which Louis won his victories and suffered his reverses.

One temporary peace was reached in 1697. But four years later hostilities were renewed on a large scale in the War of the Spanish Succession, the seed of which had been sown with Louis' marriage to Maria Theresa of Spain so many years earlier. To be brief: in 1700 Charles II, the imbecile king of Spain, died, bequeathing his imperial possessions to Philip, duke of Anjou, the grandson of Louis and Maria Theresa; Louis thereupon, and predictably, chose to regard the whole Spanish empire as a base for the extension of French power and influence; and a "grand alliance" was formed by England, Holland, and other maritime powers to frustrate his intentions—which they did. (It was during a remote extension of the international conflict that, on a winter's night in 1704, the French and their Indian allies laid waste the frontier hamlet of Deerfield in Massachusetts, burning its houses and murdering its inhabitants, or leading them away to captivity.)

The most memorable of a series of crushing defeats was administered to France by the allies at Blenheim that same year, in 1704, oddly and ironically under the leadership of Prince Eugene of Savoy, who

OVERLEAF: *Parisians enjoy pastoral pursuits on the banks of the Seine against a backdrop that includes Notre Dame and Sainte-Chapelle.*

had been refused a commission in the French army, and an English gentleman, John Churchill, duke of Marlborough, who had learned the trade of war from the most skilled of French generals. That was the beginning of the end of the Sun King's glory. When treaties of peace were signed in 1713 and 1714 the threat of French domination in Europe (or that of any other single nation) was deferred for another century—until Napoleon Bonaparte made his bid for glory, and for the glory of France.

Louis survived that last of his wars by only a year; he died in 1715. When his archenemy Eugene of Savoy heard of the king's death, he admitted that the news had the same effect on him as if he had heard of "a splendid oak uprooted and laid flat upon the ground by a storm. He had stood upright for so long!" It was too long for some. Louis' prodigalities, his dynastic wars, along with Versailles and the other elaborate constructions he decreed, had placed an oppressive burden on his subjects. By revoking the Edict of Nantes in 1685, and driving the Huguenots into exile, the king inflicted a serious wound on his own country. His Protestant victims comprised a large population of earnest, able, and prosperous citizens whom France could ill afford to lose. It was just one direct result of this tragic blunder that the silk industry of Tours was completely ruined.

Even when Louis quit Paris for Versailles and his court went with him, the great city continued to grow with added splendor of its own. During his reign the culs-de-sacs and blind alleys, known as *cours des miracles,* where criminals and outcasts had long entrenched themselves, were systematically cleaned out. More than a hundred new streets were added to the city's network, which of winter nights was lighted by sixty-five hundred lanterns. At enormous expense the place Louis le Grand was built as an administrative headquarters by Louvois around a vast octagonal space, at the center of which was installed an equestrian statue of the Sun King, cast in bronze and with its pedestal almost sixty feet high. (It is now known as the place Vendôme, its buildings occupied by the Ritz Hotel, the Ministry of Justice, large business establishments, and fashionable shops; a statue of Napoleon has long since replaced the original one.) At the personal expense of the king a magnificent new bridge, the Pont Royal, was built across the Seine, the first of the nine then standing to span the river from bank to bank

without touching one of the islands. And, as one consequence of that,
a profusion of great houses were raised in the faubourg Saint-Germain
on the Left Bank. Here it was that Marie de Médicis, discontented with
accommodations at the Louvre, had earlier constructed a large, Italian-
ate palace, long known as the Luxembourg Palace, and surrounded it
with splendid gardens that have been open to the public since 1650.

Paris remains studded with such monuments of Louis' reign—the
place des Victoires with its own statue of the king, the Hôtel Soubise
(now the National Archives), the Hôtel Carnavalet (now a historical
museum of the city of Paris), and numerous others. Most spectacular
of all is the Hôtel des Invalides with its 350-foot dome, a structure
raised over a period of thirty-five years with funds allocated from the
military budget, and dedicated by the king to the accommodation of disabled soldiers and veterans of his wars. It has been called "the capital's
most beautiful monumental group of buildings." There Napoleon was
finally entombed when his body was returned from Saint Helena.

Before Louis left the Louvre, a majestic new colonnaded facade for
that grand edifice had been planned and started, but it was not completed for more than a century to come. With the king's departure the
building was occupied by a curiously assorted population of courtiers
and poor people; its courtyards were littered with rubbish and its en-
trances converted into shops and stalls. But the new colonnade, unfinished though it was, led toward the west—toward what would become
the Champs-Élysées and the Arc de Triomphe—and that was the direction of the future development of Paris.

CHAPTER VI

TWILIGHT OF THE
ANCIENT REGIME

When he died in 1715 Louis XIV had reigned over France
for seventy-three years, longer than the lifetime of all but his most
aged subjects. Very few people then alive could have remembered the
celebrations that attended his formal coming of age in 1651, when he
was a handsome lad of thirteen and rode a spirited Spanish horse
through the streets of Paris, hat in hand, acknowledging the cheers
that greeted his progress. To one observer of that scene Louis had
seemed like a youthful Apollo—an apt comparison for the prince who
in his manhood would be so widely hailed as the Sun King and be thus
portrayed in countless gilded images.

However, before he was laid to rest, the luster of Louis' reign had
turned to a darkness that obscured the future of the nation. Louis' wars
had ended in frustration. In defeat France had not been brought to her
knees by any means, but the Great Monarch's dreams of ever-expand-
ing authority had dissolved in harsh realities. The stupendous cost of
those military ventures piled on the expenses of building and maintaining Versailles and the king's other palaces put unbearable strains on
the royal treasury. Taxes devised to carry the heavy weight of such

Mme de Pompadour, modeled in Sèvres porcelain as the goddess of love

extravagances were imposed largely on the poorer elements of the population, who were further afflicted when, twice in the latter years of Louis' rule, in 1693–94 and 1709–10, famine ravaged the land. Even earlier, in 1685 with the revocation of the Edict of Nantes and the hurried flight of the Huguenots, France had lost hundreds of thousands of its most productive people. Then, as the king aged on his throne and fought his losing wars, it was strife and starvation and disease that continued to reduce the population.

To the discontented and desperate multitudes among his subjects, Louis' death seemed like a long-anticipated release from tyrannical oppression. As the king's corpse, left to servants for disposal, was dispatched to Saint-Denis, the ancient burial place of French royalty, its passage was saluted with curses from noisy crowds that celebrated the occasion in cabarets along the way. That bitter moment closed a great era in the history of France, an era of unrivaled accomplishment and of unforgettable magnificence and, in the end, of cruel disillusionment and of virtual bankruptcy. After having elevated the monarchy to its greatest heights, Louis left it to his heirs in a state of crisis from which it would never completely recover.

Just a few years before his own death, Louis' legitimate son, his grandson, and his elder great-grandson had all died within a period of several months. Only the younger great-grandson, an ailing infant, survived in the direct line of the Bourbon succession, and it was he who, at the age of five, ascended the throne as Louis XV. By his will the dead king had almost perforce named the first prince of the blood, his nephew Philip, duke of Orléans, as regent for the youngster, although he despised and distrusted the man. By further stipulations in his will, however, he tried to rob the regent of all authority and to place his royal bastards by Mme de Montespan in effective control of the administration of the kingdom during the minority of the new little king. However, France could not be ruled from the grave. With the help of a resurgent parlement and of the aristocracy which, now that the Sun King was dead, felt it could finally throw off his despotism, Orléans had the will put aside and undertook to rule the state.

Philip of Orléans was an extremely gracious and dissipated man. He was pleased to find in himself a resemblance to the *vert galant,* Henry IV, both in his vices and in his virtues. As to the former, it is said that

Hyacinthe Rigaud's formal portrait of five-year-old Louis XV, upon his accession to the throne in 1715

he outdid his progenitor, having enjoyed the pleasure of more than a hundred mistresses in the course of his debauched life. Statistics concerning such intimacies are hardly to be trusted, but Philip's approach to those and related distractions was obvious enough, and it set a model for the new society that was re-forming in and about courtly circles. The court itself moved back from the crowded and controlled discomforts of Versailles to the freer atmosphere of Paris. Young Louis was installed with his entourage in the Tuileries at the west end of the Louvre; Philip remained nearby at the Palais Royal; the nobility built or bought their own *hôtels,* or private residences, in the city. High life in the capital quickly and gratefully forgot the rigid etiquette that had been taught at Versailles, as it cultivated the lighter modes and manners that were to prevail in royal circles until the days of reckoning two generations later.

But no degree of liberation from the old formalities, no amount of insouciance could disguise the insistent fact that the state was very close to bankruptcy. With the restoration of peace, temporary though it was, the country won back its prosperity, but the state itself was insolvent—a recurrent paradox that grew from the fruitfulness of the land and the industriousness of its people on the one hand and, on the other, the expensive penchant of the French monarchy for waging war.

In desperation over the crucial state of the royal treasury, Orléans turned for advice and help to John Law, a Scottish adventurer whose acquaintance he had made in a gambling den and who had been recommended as a bold and ingenious financier. Law, the son of an Edinburgh banker, had studied the highly developed commercial methods of Holland. (He had fled to that country some years earlier after escaping from an English jail, where he was serving a sentence for killing one Beau Wilson in a duel in Bloomsbury Square resulting from a love intrigue.) In his further travels about Europe, Law had made large sums by gambling and speculation, money which he spent with abandon. He was neither a quack nor a swindler, but a sophisticated promoter and a dauntless schemer. At the start, Law's career in France was spectacularly successful. He saw clearly enough that the nation was short of currency and that the French economy required new forms of credit to create new wealth—credit would indeed take the place of money—and he so convinced the regent of this.

From that point, the course of developments was rapid and turbulent. In the spring of 1716 Law established a private bank, which flourished; the next year he secured a trade monopoly with Louisiana, and soon thereafter with the West Indies and Canada. In 1718 his bank became a royal bank, and the year after that his Company of the West took over other old and faltering companies dealing with Africa and the East. Then Law obtained the right to collect indirect taxes within the kingdom and, ultimately, his bank took over the royal debt. In 1720 the bank and his trading company were consolidated and Law became controller general of finances of France.

To establish the credit his "system" required to succeed, Law bent his peculiar genius to attract money and people to the Mississippi valley, describing the "almost incredible advantages" of the landed concession, shares in which he peddled throughout Europe as well as in France. New Biloxi, now Biloxi, Mississippi, was to serve as a transshipping point for vast inland developments (the exploitation of mountains of precious metals and stones—gold, diamonds, emeralds —was part of the plan; Indians bedecked with gold were paraded through Paris) that would definitely and finally secure the prosperity of French empire. Lacking voluntary colonists to Louisiana, the government sent foundlings, vagabonds, criminals, and prostitutes. Selling shares in the enterprise was another matter. The excitement aroused by the wildly speculative entrepreneur could hardly be contained. Law himself was all but assaulted by investors eager to come close to the very source of such quick profits; he had regal power in his hands; the exiled Stuarts of England paid him court; and the rue Quincampoix in Paris, center of the stockjobbing, became a scene of pandemonium as frantic investors pressed their claims for shares.

Then, in December, 1720, Law's "Mississippi Bubble," blown up to fantastic proportions, burst. Fortunes that had been made on paper were suddenly worthless, and Law and all his schemes were castigated in an outpouring of unbridled invective. At Biloxi half the colonists died and the rest sat at the shore watching for ships that it seemed would never come to relieve their plight. (In *Manon Lescaut,* the famous novel by the Abbé Prévost, the heroine, a courtesan, was thus transported to America, where she died, transformed by love and suffering, in the arms of the devoted lover who had followed her there.)

A contemporary engraving depicting the panic on the rue Quincampoix, in Paris, following the collapse of John Law's "Mississippi Bubble"

Law left France poorer than he found it, although that apparently did not alter his faith in the promise of his system. Montesquieu, who visited him in Venice after the debacle, described the inveterate but impoverished schemer as still dreaming of vast projects that would return him to power and France to prosperity.

In 1718, as one by-product of Law's dreams and the great excitement of the times, the Crescent City of New Orleans had been founded by one of the first acts of the directors of his company. Four years later the little town was made the capital of the Louisiana Colony, a community long since grown into an important and picturesque city that, born as it was of such extraordinary circumstances, has never forgotten its French heritage.

The person mainly responsible for the economic recovery of France following the Law debacle was a frugal, prudent, overtly unassuming septuagenarian, André Hercule de Fleury, bishop of Fréjus and the young king's beloved tutor. He came to authority only after a succession of events paved the way. Orléans died in 1723 and his authority was assumed by the one-eyed, bow-legged, and stupid duke of Bourbon, who was the next prince of the blood. To secure succession of the Bourbon dynasty in direct line, the duke looked for a fruitful wife for the king, although the monarch was only fifteen. First the Spanish infanta was summoned, but she was a mere child and was hurried back to Spain after a severe illness had threatened Louis' life—a turnabout that infuriated the Spanish court. Next a marriage was arranged for the boy king with Maria Leszczyńska, daughter of Stanislas I, former king of Poland. Maria was no beauty, but she was twenty-one, healthy, and glad to be wanted. The two were married in 1725, and the first of their seven children was born in 1729. (Although the Polish princess soon bored Louis, she gently complained that he was always taking her to bed, albeit "without addressing a word to her"; and soon Louis also took to bed the first in a series of mistresses.)

Then Bourbon overplayed his hand by trying to use the queen to remove Fleury from his position of influence near the king, who had become officially of age when he was thirteen. Faithful to his old friend, Louis banished Bourbon and his pretty mistress from court circles. Since the king was lazy, indifferent, and inexperienced, Fleury took over the administration of his kingdom and remained in that office until he died in 1743 at the age of ninety. The old tutor had been made a cardinal and, like his illustrious predecessors, Richelieu and Mazarin, he gave France a working government. By cautious diplomacy, in close personal understanding with Sir Robert Walpole in England, Fleury worked for peace, which France so sorely needed. He reordered the fiscal affairs of the state, stabilized its currency, and restored its prosperity—for a while. In 1733 Fleury was virtually forced into a war to support the efforts of the queen's father, Stanislas Leszczyński, to reclaim the throne of Poland. That gambit did not succeed, but in the peace signed in 1735 a happy compromise was reached; Stanislas was given instead the throne of Lorraine, a territory that was to revert to France upon his death (which it did in 1766).

Both before and after Fleury's death France was to suffer more costly wars. But at least the country was spared invasion, and it remained free of civil strife until, late in the century, the revolution erupted that shook the world. With a quarter of a century of peace on the high seas, French commerce expanded and the merchant marine was rejuvenated. Such ports as Marseilles, Dunkirk, Le Havre, Nantes, La Rochelle, and Bordeaux flourished and, with their increased prosperity, took on new character. As a prime example, the merchants and traders of Bordeaux, exploiting outlets both to the Atlantic through the great estuary of the Gironde and, by means of the Canal du Midi, to the Mediterranean and the Levant, amassed wealth enough to transform their medieval port into a handsome, "modern" eighteenth-century city. The rewards of peace and industry in new building and planning found expression everywhere. In Lorraine, under the temporary rule of Stanislas, Nancy became one of the most beautiful small capitals of Europe, a model of urban planning and a jewel of eighteenth-century architecture. Its main square, surrounded by impressive buildings, is still closed off by four magnificent gilded wrought-iron screens designed by Jean Lamour, a virtuoso blacksmith of the time.

Although the court returned to Versailles, money merchants became kings of Paris in their own fashion, and built accordingly. In 1718 the count of Évreux, son-in-law of the great financier Crozat (who, before Law, had held a monopoly in trade with Louisiana), built a majestic house in the faubourg Saint-Honoré on the western outskirts of the city, a structure that survived the intervening years to become known

One of the rococo wrought-iron grilles designed around 1751 by Jean Lamour for the corners of the place Stanislas in Nancy

(since 1873), as the Élysée palace, the residence of the presidents of the republic of France. Five times in forty years Louis XV tried by edict to restrict new building beyond the strict limits of Paris, to prevent too-rapid expansion of the city; but that did little good. In Paris, as elsewhere, with a long term of internal peace and with an increasing population, city limits earlier defined by fortified ramparts had already been exceeded. As the obsolete fortifications were pulled down, the way was opened for the development of the *grands boulevards* that would channel so much of the spirited life of Paris in years to come.

As did other French cities, Paris planned and built its *place royale* to honor Louis XV in regal fashion, a large square laid out at the western limits of the Garden of the Tuileries—on waste space, beyond which extended a wooded path that led through the Champs-Élysées to the open country beyond. The place Louis XV, later renamed place de la Révolution, and then called place de la Concorde, covers one hundred thousand square yards; it took twenty years to complete; with its statuary, fountains, and esplanade it is possibly the most celebrated urban space in the world. At the north side two magnificent identical structures, divided by the rue Royale, were raised to house some members of the nobility and to serve as state offices. They are among the finest architectural examples of the period; today, one serves as headquarters for the Ministry of the Marine and the other has become the luxurious Hôtel Crillon.

During Fleury's administration of the state, the population of France was rapidly increasing. So it was generally in Europe in the eighteenth century, but until late in that century France remained, as it had long been, the most populous nation of the Western world. The prosperity apparent in the ports and large cities was, however, neither broadly nor evenly distributed. Through traditional rights and privileges and by devious means and methods, sizeable numbers of Frenchmen managed to escape direct taxation, leaving an increased burden on the others—principally and most unhappily on the peasantry. Yet even the peasantry may have been better off than it sometimes seemed. In his *Confessions,* for example, the philosopher Jean Jacques Rousseau told of a stop he had made, tired and hungry, at a country house, where at first he was offered the most meager fare; but when it was learned that he was not an agent of the tax gatherer, as had been feared, his relieved

host provided an ample meal of meat, eggs, bread, and wine drawn
from hidden resources. (Voltaire went so far as to say there was no
country in the world where the farmer was better off.)

For those who had to pay them, the indirect taxes that were imposed
were just as vexatious—and infinitely complex in their application.
The tax on salt, the hated *gabelle,* was steadily increased during the
century, until the Revolution, and was imposed with a wide variety of
rates throughout the realm. Smuggling salt, consequently, became almost an industry, and the harsh measures taken to suppress that activity led to further discontents. Domestic trade was also subject to
excise taxes, with innumerable customs barriers set up to collect the
fees due on various commodities passing from one province to another.
As a result, there was still more smuggling within the country. All the
efforts of Colbert, in the name of the most absolute of monarchs, had
failed to standardize and unify rules, laws, and procedures in the face
of entrenched local rights and privileges. Even such vital and elementary matters as weights and measures were subject to wide variation
from region to region. A "league" might be considered the equivalent
of 2,000 yards in one place and of 3,000 yards elsewhere. There was no
such thing as a common measure for a carafe of wine. Every part of the
land had its own particular and customary laws, which might vary even
from one village to the next. "In France," as Voltaire remarked, "a
traveler changes his laws as often as he changes his horses."

In spite of having to depend on such cumbersome and inefficient
methods of raising revenue and administering the government, by his
pacific and cautious policies Fleury had managed to extricate France
from the almost disastrous consequences of Law's failure. By 1738 the
national debt had at long last been turned into a surplus. His achievement gave the monarchy a reprieve that Louis hardly appreciated; no
matter what the state of the economy and the treasury, the gross extravagances of the court continued unabated. Fleury was now aging
and his powers rapidly waning. In 1741, unable to resist the pressures
from his marshals and his mistresses, and discarding Fleury's counsel,
Louis allowed France to drift into the first of a series of wars which
immediately started a crucial drain on the French treasury.

Eventually all the great European powers were drawn into the conflict. The first phase of the drawn-out struggle, remembered as the War

of the Austrian Succession, started when Frederick the Great seized
Silesia from Austria with the aim of establishing the house of Hohenzollern as a rival to the Hapsburgs in the domination of Germany.
France became involved, first as Frederick's ally, then as his enemy, in
an ill-considered attempt on the part of Louis' militant advisers to
revive the glorious days of Louis XIV. England saw this as another
bid for French hegemony in Europe and, prompted by the additional
fact that George II was also elector of Hanover, Prussia's neighbor,
quickly joined the fray. Others, including Russia, took to arms on one
side or the other. (In America, where the struggle was known as King
George's War, untrained troops from the English colonies captured
the French fortress at Louisbourg, the so-called Canadian Gibraltar.)

Fleury's voice was all but stilled. In 1743, at a moment when the
French armies were in retreat, the grieving old man died in office—and
in his second childhood. No one took his place. Louis presumed to be
his own prime minister like Louis XIV before him, but he had neither
the strength of mind nor will to meet such responsibilities, and he fell
into the hands of advisers who differed among themselves, leaving him
irresolute. At the council table, one of them wrote, Louis "opened his
mouth, said little and thought not at all." That was a harsh judgment
from a bitter critic. The king had wit and intelligence enough but, as
another contemporary observed, his modesty was pushed to the extreme of a vice; and this and other defects of his character played a
dominating role in the government of France for the next twenty years.

The weary conflict dragged on with intermittent truces until the in-
conclusive peace of Aix-la-Chapelle briefly terminated hostilities in
1748. France won some notable victories on land, but in the end gained
nothing from them. Prussia, however, emerged as an important power
among the German states, with grave portents for the future of France.
And England, on the strength of her naval conquests, assumed new
authority on the high seas. (By the terms of the peace treaty Louisbourg was returned to France for the time.) What followed was another uneasy truce.

In global perspective the war in Germany was part of a world-wide
struggle for empire between France and England. The next phase in
that contest broke out in the American colonies, two years before either
country was again embroiled in German affairs. In North America the

The philosophe *Voltaire, candidly conceived in marble by Jean Houdon*

bloody French and Indian wars were starting again (actually, they had never stopped). On Christmas 1753 the young George Washington, guided by friendly Indians, carried a note from Governor Dinwiddie at Williamsburg, Virginia, to the French commander at Fort LeBoeuf in what is now western Pennsylvania, expressing astonishment that he was occupying territory "so notoriously known to be the property of the Crown of Great Britain." The note was rebuffed with Gallic courtesy and military firmness. A year later Washington was back on the frontier to insist upon English claims. There followed a brief but important skirmish in which Washington's improvised militia was defeated. Of that skirmish Voltaire wrote, "Such was the complications of political interests that a cannon shot fired in America could give the signal that set Europe in blaze." Thus, in the wilderness of the American West, started the Seven Years' War.

Once again most of the nations of Europe took to arms—France, Austria, Russia, Saxony, Sweden, and Spain on the one side and Prussia, Hanover, and Great Britain on the other. After a promising beginning, with victories both by land and by sea, French fortunes were reversed at every quarter. Finally, in 1763, war-weary and financially depleted, France signed a humiliating treaty of peace with Great Britain, giving up all claims to Canada (Voltaire sneeringly referred to that large and rich land as "a few acres of snow"), all the vast territory between the Appalachian Mountains and the Mississippi River (in which area the war had been sparked), and islands in the West Indies. Louisiana was ceded to Spain to compensate for the loss of Florida. French possessions in India were reduced to a few trading stations. And French prestige in Europe was all but destroyed. On the other hand, Great Britain emerged from the war as the world's major colonial empire and as mistress of the seas; Prussia was established as a leading European power; and Russia had made its first serious intrusion into purely European affairs.

The earlier of those wars that ended so miserably for France was at midpoint when Louis' current mistress died (she was the third in a series of sisters who thus served him), and the king quite literally fell into the arms of a *petite bourgeoise* whom he installed at Versailles as the marquise de Pompadour. For almost twenty years this witty, pretty, and urbane *parvenue* remained the king's confidante, a "prime min-

This detail of François Boucher's "Toilette of Venus" reflects the sensuality of French court life.

ister in petticoats," as she was derisively called by those who deplored her influence. She corresponded regularly with the generals of the army in the field; and it was long believed that she altered France's traditional alliances with the German states against Austria because Frederick the Great of Prussia lampooned her in verse and Maria Theresa of Austria wrote her a friendly letter—a shift in old friends and enemies that brought on the disasters of the Seven Years' War. But this is to exaggerate the importance of her privileged and intimate role by the king's side.

Pompadour is more happily and more reliably remembered for her lavish but discerning patronage of the arts and letters of her time. During the years of her influence, and with her encouragement, the Louis XV style with all its delicacy and grace was brought to its ultimate degree of refinement. Everything about that style expressly rejected the rigidly formal patterns that had been imposed at Versailles under the regime of Louis XIV. As just one example of a new spirit of liberation, chairs that had been straight-backed and thronelike, lined against the wall like so many immovable symbols of *place,* now took a wide variety of graceful forms with such suggestive names as *bergère* (or "shepherd's chair"), *gondole, confidante,* and so on. Curvilinear designs of the rococo style gave an effect of life and movement to such seating devices, which were indeed meant to be moved—to be pulled about for comfort and to facilitate sitting in those small, intimate conversational groups that played a vital part in the social and intellectual life of France in the closing decades of the *ancien régime.* And all other domestic arrangements were also designed to further comfort, convenience, privacy, and intimacy.

The porcelain factory at Sèvres, just outside Paris, was founded at Pompadour's instigation to match the exquisite fabrications of the Meissen works in Germany. With her approval the Gobelins, Beauvais, and Aubusson factories continued to receive the royal patronage that enabled them to produce tapestries of unexcelled quality. She personally frequented the shops of craftsmen along the fashionable rue Saint-Honoré and, with her all but unlimited budget, bought there and elsewhere such an abundance of treasures that upon her death it took two notaries an entire year to catalogue her possessions. It was at the height of her influence that the plans were drawn for the place de la Concorde.

Her brother Marigny, the king's superintendent of buildings, contributed much to the elegance of the contemporary architectural scene.

The marquise had some artistic talents of her own and to develop them she chose as a tutor, and as her favorite painter, another bourgeois, François Boucher, an artist who designed objects for the Sèvres factory, drew cartoons for tapestries, and among other things did sets for the opera and ballet. In his paintings Boucher lacked the poetic genius of Jean Antoine Watteau, whose canvases of haunting, dreamlike beauty, painted in the years just before and after the death of Louis XIV, had departed so dramatically from the grand and heavy manner favored by the Sun King. But Boucher was the perfect painter for Pompadour and her courtly circle. It has been said that he brought the gods into the boudoir and bedroom, with his brush transmuting Venus, Diana, and their attendants into nubile and seductive grisettes. Well connected and capable as he was, Boucher was named painter to the king and president of the Academy.

There were other successful and talented contemporary artists. To name but two highly disparate but brilliant examples, there were Jean Honoré Fragonard, who with his happy and luscious confections became the darling of the demimonde; and Jean Baptiste Siméon Chardin, whose unsentimentalized pictures of simple people going about their simple domestic routines and whose still lifes were the very opposite of "Frago's" frivolities. But years later the brothers de Goncourt wrote that it was Boucher who expressed, personified, and embodied the taste of the eighteenth century "in all the peculiarity of its character." In Boucher's own lifetime Denis Diderot, the philosopher and *encyclopédist,* assailed the artist for doing just that—at least for suggesting the depravity, dissoluteness, and debauchery that characterized life among the members of the *haut monde* who commissioned his paintings. Where in all this, asked Diderot, were ideas of honesty, innocence, and simplicity? The answer was all too obvious to critics of such a society.

The critics of society spoke with many voices. Never before in history had man in the name of reason so thoroughly examined the nature of the human condition, the structure of his institutions, and the relations of man to man. This would indeed be known as the Age of Reason, or the Age of Enlightenment as it is also called. During the reign of Louis XIV there had been little open questioning of established, traditional, and orthodox authority, although in their writings Pascal, Descartes, Rabelais, Montaigne, and others had sown seeds of scepticism that were carefully nurtured in the years that followed. Shortly after the Sun King died, in the somewhat more relaxed and permissive days of the Regency, Montesquieu published his *Lettres persanes* ("Persian Letters"), a satire and criticism of French institutions in the guise of letters purportedly written or received by two Persians traveling in France and commenting on the scene with astonishment. That publication won Montesquieu immediate notoriety.

A few years later, after a highly rewarding exile in England, Voltaire published his *Lettres anglaises* in which by praising virtually everything English he implicitly attacked the establishment of state and church in France. (It has been said that Voltaire was "England's best gift to France.") Montesquieu as well as Voltaire found in the English experience—in the "glorious revolution" of 1688, in the writings of Newton, Locke, and others, and in the tolerant atmosphere of English society—a model France might well emulate. "Here is a country," wrote Voltaire, "where a man can think freely and nobly, without being hindered by any servile fear." England, on the other hand, read with avid interest what French writers were producing. Culturally the two nations were never closer than in this century when they were so often at war with one another. It was under the sign of that interplay of ideas and influence that the United States of America was born.

About the middle of the eighteenth century, there followed an abundant crop of new and radical publications that in effect proclaimed a revolution in ideas. The books came out in rapid succession, neglecting few aspects of human experience from their scrutiny. In 1748 Montesquieu published *De l'esprit des lois,* in which he analyzed different kinds of political regimes and condemned the abuses of the monarchical system in France. (The Founding Fathers of the United States quoted Montesquieu with reverence.) The first volume of Buffon's *Histoire naturelle* appeared in 1749, and in that work the great naturalist included opinions and speculation that in some cases anticipated the conclusions of Darwin. In 1750 Rousseau issued his *Discours sur les sciences et les arts* in which, considering the effect of civilization's progress on morals, he developed his celebrated contention that man

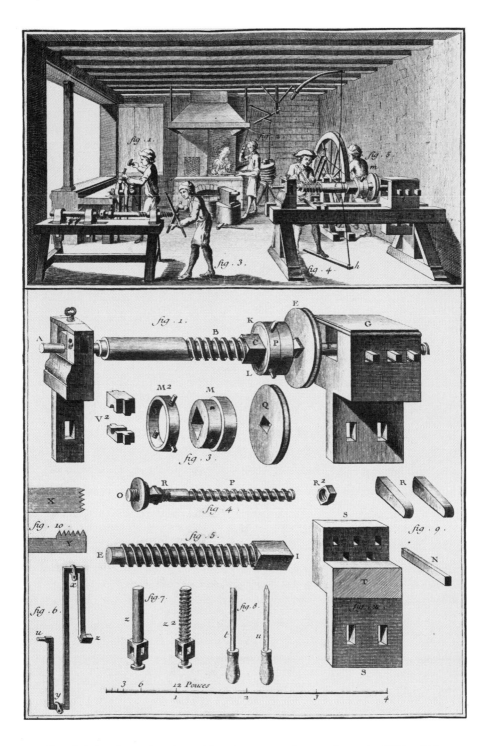

Detailed drawings of tools used in a press-screw factory, from the 1771 supplement of Diderot's L'Encyclopédie

was best off in a "natural," primitive state; twelve years later he wrote his most famous book, *The Social Contract.* Voltaire, D'Alembert, Condorcet, Diderot, and others of the so-called *philosophes* added to this flowering of rational inquiry which brought above the surface and into the open controversies that had earlier largely forced their way underground.

The single most important publication in this outgrowth of free thought was undoubtedly Diderot's monumental *L'Encyclopédie,* the first volume of which appeared in 1751 and which included contributions from the authors mentioned above and a constellation of other brilliant minds. Its success was instant and its influence immeasurable, for it embodied all the advanced thought of the century, presented under a veneer of commonplace information. Because it called attention to abuses of the clergy and officialdom it was twice suppressed (and Diderot was repeatedly imprisoned), but it nevertheless found its way to a surprisingly wide public. "Whenever the King sought information, whether on the formula for gunpowder or that for lip rouge," wrote André Maurois, "Madame de Pompadour had a copy of the forbidden work brought for his consultation. The King would find what he was looking for and regret the suppression."

Pompadour supported Diderot, Voltaire, and others associated with the *Encyclopédie* against their reactionary enemies at court. (Voltaire, who earlier had twice been thrown into the Bastille for his intransigent writing, owed his election to the Academy to Pompadour's protection.) But she could not transform the king into such an enlightened despot as Frederick the Great and Catherine of Russia presumed to be, both of whom were friendly admirers of the French intellectuals and shared their interests.

The French court remained dull and depraved. The brightest minds and most adventurous spirits of France found their own private courts in the salons of Mme Geoffrin, Mme du Deffand, Mlle de Lespinasse, and other brilliant ladies who made virtually an institution of their intimate gatherings. Horace Walpole, Stanislas I (the future king of Poland), Baron von Grimm, and other impressively distinguished foreigners were the sometime guests of such groups, as were Louis' chief ministers and other members of French officialdom and of the Church. Although badinage and flirtation were essential to these ostensibly social occasions, there was also serious and stimulating conversation in which lucid presentation of the most abstruse topics was carefully cultivated—a discipline that had a beneficent influence on French writing then and in the years to come.

There was no end to conversation. The *philosophes* also met at the cafés of Paris to hold forth and exchange views. Rousseau could be seen at the Café de la Veuve Laurent on the rue Dauphine, Maupertuis and others at the Café Gradot on the quai de l'École, and Voltaire, Diderot, Fontenelle, and still others at the Café Procope, the most famous of those *café littéraires* and still standing on the rue de l'Ancienne-Comédie. It was said that the coffee as it was prepared and served at the Café Procope sent a man away feeling he had four times the spirit he had when he arrived.

In the words of Mme de Lambert, whose salon was one of the earliest of the century, to philosophize was "to shake off the yoke of authority." To what degree the writings of the *philosophes* helped to precipitate the French Revolution has been argued about ever since 1789. Long before their work was completed, Pompadour had made her sinister prophecy, *après nous le déluge* ("after us the deluge"). Her own influence, for good and for bad, ceased with her death in 1764 at the age of forty-three. When she learned that the end was imminent, she proudly dressed herself in full court costume and expired in style. As her body was taken away from Versailles in the midst of a violent storm, Louis watched from a balcony and cried. He had long since dismissed her as a bedmate, but she had accepted and befriended her more enticing successors, and she had ever retained Louis' confidence and his trust. But the people of France were not moved to tears when she died; she was too closely associated with the costly excesses of the court, with its flagrant immorality, and with wars and taxes.

Twenty years before, in a brief moment of popularity, the king had been fondly nicknamed the Well-Beloved by his subjects. However, that sentiment passed. Just a few years later Louis felt obliged to build a special road to take him between Fontainebleau and Versailles without passing through Paris, where he feared a bad reception. In 1747 an attempt was even made on the king's life, which apparently astounded no one but Louis himself. When he died of smallpox in 1774 he went to his grave unlamented, if not without comment. As his funeral cor-

OVERLEAF: *the poor people of Paris frolic on the eve of the Revolution*

tege moved toward his burial place, the story went, it was greeted with cynical comments from the roadside observers.

From the conclusion of the Seven Years' War to the day of Louis' death, and beyond, France's crying need was for some reform of royal finances, and for the restoration of royal authority that would make such reform possible. In both matters the king and his ministers were checked by the parlements whose primary and traditional function was the administration of justice throughout the realm but whose claims to sovereign authority had never been completely relinquished. The parlement of Paris had demonstrated such authority in 1763 when they obliged Louis, against his disposition to do so, to issue a royal edict abolishing the Society of Jesus, confiscating its property, and dispersing its members. (What effect the suppression of Jesuit teachers, and their replacement by laymen on members of minor orders, may have had on the minds of the generation that came of age with the Revolution can only be conjectured.) Largely to safeguard their own privileged status the members of parlement also blocked any efforts by the royal government toward fiscal reform. Louis finally realized that either he or the parlements must rule France and, stirred out of his habitual apathy, in 1771 he simply abolished those hereditary bodies and sent their members into exile. ("For myself, I think the king is right," Voltaire remarked, "and since it is necessary to serve, I would rather do so under a lion of good pedigree . . . than under two hundred rats of my own kind.") But Louis had little time left to recapture lost ground before he died in 1774.

Louis XVI was barely twenty when he succeeded to the throne. At sixteen, to re-enforce the Austrian alliance, he had been married to the archduchess Marie Antoinette. France welcomed the youthful couple, who provided a remarkable and refreshing contrast to the lecherous rake and the compliant mistresses who had preceded them. This young Louis truly wanted to be loved by his people, but he was utterly incapable of governing them or of guiding their destiny. While the young king spent happy hours riding to the hunt and practicing locksmithing, France headed toward revolution. Hoping to accomplish through parlement what he could not succeed in doing by royal edict alone, Louis recalled that traditional body that his grandfather had dismissed. The monarchy thereupon lost its last chance of achieving sol-

vency—and of controlling its own destiny. The returned parlements
struck down every effort of the royal ministers to reform the finances
of the realm, now in a more crucial state than ever. And by their defiance of royal edicts those privileged bodies set an example for their
unprivileged countrymen of resistance to the rightful authority of the
king. It is ironic, but not surprising, that their privileges were among
the first casualties of the revolution toward which they themselves
helped pave the way.

It is another and much more striking irony that in supporting the
cause of American freedom the French monarchy virtually committed
unintentional suicide. Ever since the miserable defeats of the Seven
Years' War, important factions in the French government had hoped
and planned for revenge against the English. At great expense the
navy had been rebuilt and massively enlarged and the army reconstituted. Regular troops were recruited and trained to replace the old
militia. Scholarships were provided at military schools for the sons of
poor nobles to learn the arts of war. (One recipient was to be a lad
named Bonaparte.) The artillery was reformed into the most modern
and effective one in Europe. France was ready to challenge England
once again. And the American Revolution provided an opportunity
that could hardly be denied.

First almost surreptitiously, then, following the surprising American victory over the British at Saratoga in 1777, openly and in generous
measure, France joined that struggle. The results are common knowledge. In 1780–81 Rochambeau's armies and Admiral de Grasse's fleet
made certain the final British surrender at Yorktown. England had
been humiliated; France had emerged from the conflict as a champion
of human freedom, and demonstrably a formidable power once again
on land and sea. French prestige was never higher. France was still the
most populous country in the Western world. Its artists, architects,
and writers were renowned in all quarters of Europe and America. But
France was now bankrupt. And Frenchmen had seen how Benjamin
Franklin and his countrymen—with the help of their allies to be sure—
could "snatch the scepter from the hands of tyrants." The lesson was
not lost, as subsequent events demonstrated.

CHAPTER VII

THE GREAT
STORM

*L*ouis XVI was anything but a tyrant. He was in fact just the opposite, a king with not enough will to rule. There was no need or reason to snatch the scepter from his hands; it virtually dropped from his faltering fingers as he was jostled by circumstances he could neither understand nor control. After centuries of erratic growth since the day of Hugh Capet, the French monarchy had become an institution of awesome majesty under Louis XIV. But the two following reigns had largely dissipated that inheritance. Quite aside from the question of temporal power, the divine right of the king to rule, so naturally conceded to Saint Louis five centuries earlier in an age of faith, was all but unthinkable in the Age of Reason with Louis XVI on the throne. (In his great work, *De l'esprit des lois,* in which he searchingly questioned the nature of government, Montesquieu had not even bothered to consider the matter.) The Bourbon dynasty was both materially and spiritually bankrupt. On the fourteenth of July, 1789, when the Paris mobs stormed the Bastille, the king entered the single word "Nothing" in his diary, indicating the results of a poor day's hunting.

Talleyrand once remarked that whoever had not lived before 1789

Louis XVI, as painted in his full regal attire by Duplessis had not known "the sweetness of life." Compared with the turbulence of the revolutionary period that followed, those earlier years must indeed have seemed pleasant to remember. Life at Versailles, geared to royal indulgence, was obviously undisturbed by premonitions of any serious change in routine, let alone of disasters, that would end forever the *ancien régime*. The people of France were not hostile to their monarch. He may no longer have been hedged by divinity, but in theory and by old tradition his rule was still absolute; he was at least the source of ultimate authority. Over and again in past crises—after the wars of religion, after the *Fronde,* and at other times of trouble—the nation had turned to the king to heal its wounds and restore its well-being, to reform abuses and control the sources of feudal privilege—to maintain a sovereign state, which had always seemed best in the end. As a symbol, at least, Louis remained the hope of his subjects until at last his credit was altogether exhausted by the demands made upon it.

As the decade of the 1780s ran its course, most of the people of France wanted changes in the government not because their lot was miserable—they were in fact relatively well off (so long as the harvests were ample)—but because they saw good reasons why it should be improved. The country was prosperous. It required only changes in management to open the doors of advancement and opportunity to those who were qualified for better things in life. Lafayette, who had served a revolutionary cause in America, thought that the necessary changes could be made in France without recourse to violence. "French affairs," he explained in a letter to George Washington, "are the harder to resolve because the people of that country seem in no way ready to turn to extreme measures. 'Liberty or death' is not a fashionable motto on this side of the Atlantic." However, that was precisely the choice forced upon Lafayette himself just a few years later amid scenes of violence.

The currents of history run fitfully. At some points they turn sluggish, spreading out into what seem like stagnant pools of time, as in the so-called Dark Ages. At other points they appear to rush on, cutting new channels toward the future, as they did, for instance, in the early years of the sixteenth century. In 1789, with the storming of the Bastille, the flow of human events suddenly broke into a rapids which in its swirling, turbulent course had no precedent. Madame de Pompadour's cynical prophecy, *après nous le déluge,* had barely hinted at the floods that were in fact released by the fall of the old regime in France. For a quarter of a century, ending with the maelstrom at Waterloo in 1815, peoples and principalities were tossed about by forces that shattered the peace of Europe and disrupted its established structure. Within those relatively few years radical changes took place in French society and French government—changes whose impact reached to the far corners of the world with revolutionary consequences. This was, as Thomas Carlyle wrote in his *French Revolution,* "a cup of trembling which all nations shall drink."

Carlyle's book and Charles Dickens' *Tale of Two Cities* have left two dramatic accounts of the Revolution that will probably forever color the imagination of the English-reading public. However, neither such misleading romances nor the more disciplined studies of scholars have provided any conclusive explanation of just why France erupted when and as it did. That cataclysmic episode gave rise to conflicting currents of thought and action that can hardly be fully explored or neatly summarized in a few pages and that are still under debate.

It would be too simple to claim that revolution was the price France paid for American independence. Yet the disturbances in France did stem in good part from debts the French government incurred by supporting America's revolt against England. Every effort by Louis XVI's ministers to replenish the national coffers through tax reforms continued to be frustrated by the parlements, whose members enjoyed exemptions and privileges they were not prepared to yield—a stand in which they were supported by members of the nobility who were no less eager to retain their own exemptions. But only by such reforms could the royal government manage to gain access to the country's substantial wealth.

Now the privileged classes that for so long had sown the wind were about to reap the whirlwind. They had in effect revolted against the king's authority and would have to pay the consequences. Forced by desperate circumstances to extreme measures the monarchy convened the Estates General at Versailles. That body, made up of representatives of the three orders—the clergy, the nobility, and the Third Estate, or commons—had first been assembled in 1302 to support the policies of Philip IV, but it had not been called together for the last 175 years,

OVERLEAF: *"The Oath of the Tennis Court" at Versailles, June 22, 1789*

while the monarchy continued to survive its varying difficulties without recourse to such counsel and support.

By custom the three orders of the Estates General had debated and voted by class order, and consent of all three was necessary to bind their recommendations. That virtually gave the nobility a veto power over any reform that did not serve its special interests. However, the Third Estate constituted roughly 98 per cent of the population of the land. In fact and in law it included in its numbers the bourgeois, those middle-class business and professional men, landowners, officials, and other consequential persons who had risen to positions of large and increasing influence since the Estates had last been summoned. And now it was their move to take over the revolution that had been initiated by the aristocracy. "Those who gave the first impulse," wrote Robespierre, in retrospect, "have long since repented, or at least wished to stop the revolution when they saw that the people might recover its sovereignty. But it was they who started it. Without their resistance, and their mistaken calculations, the nation would still be under the yoke of despotism."

On May 4, 1789, when the Estates General met, the members of the Third Estate were obliged to enter the assembly hall by a side door after the clergy and nobles had passed through the front. Louis, "gorgeous as Solomon in all his glory," as Carlyle described the monarch, addressed his audience "with sonorous tone" and "conceivable speech. . . ." (Thomas Jefferson, who was present, thought that the king spoke impressively; that, "viewed as an opera," it was an imposing scene.) "But there is endless discrepancy round him," Carlyle continued; "so many claims and clamours; a mere confusion of tongues. Not reconcilable by man; not manageable, suppressible, save by some strongest and wisest man; for France at large, hitherto mute, is now beginning to speak also."

That particular spring France was speaking with a special sense of grievance from all the countryside where, because of a bad harvest the year before, grain was scarce and the price of bread was high. The winter of 1788–89 had been the coldest in memory (in Paris the temperature sank to 20 degrees below zero), which seriously aggravated the grain shortage. Even the wealthiest hosts had advised their guests to bring their own bread to dinner. To a very large part of the population this was a cause of acute distress, and, as summer approached, there were riots throughout the land. It was a real and immediate issue to be coped with. When it became apparent that the king's ministers had no intention of listening to the special complaints of the representatives of the commanding majority of the French people, but rather were prepared to accept a program of minimal reform proposed by the aristocracy, the Third Estate set up a separate National Assembly. Since the hall that had been reserved for their meetings was, quite casually, closed to them—and the building occupied by royal troops—the members adjourned through a pouring rain, to a nearby covered tennis court, and there took an oath—the famous Oath of the Tennis Court—not to separate until they had given the realm a constitution; and in this purpose they were joined by a number of the clergy and some of the nobility who were sympathetic with their aims. When the king's master of ceremonies commanded the Assembly to withdraw, the count of Mirabeau (a noble from Provence with a notorious past who had been elected as a representative of the Third Estate) retorted in the name of the people that there would be no withdrawal save at bayonet's point. And to that defiant statement all the king could or did say was, in effect, "They want to stay? Well, damn it, let them!"—and he "commanded" the three orders to reconvene, which they finally did as a Constitutional Assembly. The court had practically capitulated to the people of France.

Some optimists thought the Revolution was already all over. "Now we are allowed to hope," Mirabeau remarked, "that we are beginning the history of man." But the Assembly had set in motion forces that it could not control; and the king stumbled from one predicament to another. Rumors spread about Paris that Louis had summoned several regiments of his army to that area and it was then, as if by reflex action, that the Parisian mobs stormed and destroyed the Bastille. In itself this was not an incident of major consequence, but it became and it remains a symbol of the collapse of the old order. It was reported to the king the next day, after he had rested from his fruitless hunting the day before. "Why, that is a revolt," poor Louis expostulated. "Sire," he was answered, "it is not a revolt—it is a revolution."

Actually it was not even a revolt; it was only a big riot. But elsewhere in France there were more bread riots and agrarian uprisings,

A scene of violence at the storming of the Bastille, July 14, 1789

chateaux were put to the torch and feudal landlords terrorized. Three
weeks after the demolition of the Bastille the nobles and the clergy in
the Assembly, partly in fear, partly in recognition of the urgent needs
of the moment, relinquished all their ancient and timeworn privileges.
In one night, August 4, 1789, the entire remaining feudal structure of
France was abolished. Later that same month, on August 26, the Assembly issued a Declaration of the Rights of Man and the Citizen,
intended as a preface to the constitution it was preparing for the nation,
which was reluctantly approved by the king. That document was a bill
of rights compounded from precedents earlier established in England
and America and from the theories of the *philosophes*. Through it the
aspirations of the great reformers of the Enlightenment—of Locke,
Jefferson, Montesquieu, Rousseau, and others—were transmitted to
revolutionaries in Europe for generations to come.

But it brought no immediate settlement to the general unrest. Early
in October a riotous mob, with a core of hard-bitten women from Les
Halles, marched out from Paris to Versailles, some twelve miles away,
through mud and rain, to demand bread. They were about seven thousand strong and they dragged cannon along with them. Warned of
their advance, Louis returned early from his hunting that day and
granted an interview to a delegation of the marchers. Bread was promised, but there were ugly episodes. Marie Antoinette barely escaped
from her bedroom with her life. Lafayette arrived late at night at the
head of an army of twenty thousand men, including the newly formed
National Guard accompanied by further armed crowds, to control the
situation and to "invite" Louis back to Paris. The caravan that trekked
back to the city the next day was a curious mixture of jubilant, bedrag-
gled market women, garlanded with oak and poplar, disarmed royal
troops, the royal family, carriages filled with deputies, all attended by
Lafayette and his National Guard. They had been preceded by an advance contingent bearing aloft as trophies the severed heads of two of
Louis' bodyguards. Louis returned at last to the long-abandoned palace
of the Tuileries.

For the next five years Paris, with its mobs as a handy weapon for
whatever faction could manage to direct them, and with king and Assembly in the city's custody, prescribed the course of the Revolution.
But the kingdom was in desperate straits; its finances and administra-

tion both needed prompt reorganization. To meet the latter problem, under the new constitution, the ancient provinces—Burgundy, Normandy, Brittany, and the others from which the kingdom had been pieced together over the centuries and which retained close associations with the *ancien régime*—were replaced by eighty-three smaller units, or *départements*—divisions named after rivers and mountains—which, it was hoped, would restore the natural areas and boundaries of local life in French government. To avert complete and imminent bankruptcy the lands held by the Church—about one fifth of the territory of France—were nationalized and used as credit for the issue of paper currency in the form of *assignats*. Priests were made public officials, elected by the people and paid by the state; as public servants they were required to take an oath of fidelity to the constitution; a war between church and state had been started and would continue to the twentieth century.

Under those circumstances, on the night of June 20, 1791, Louis and his royal family slipped out of the Tuileries and fled eastward toward

The women from Les Halles on their way to Versailles, October 5, 1789

the frontier where aristocratic French émigrés had earlier taken refuge and were scheming to form a coalition against the revolutionaries. The story is well known; as he approached the border the king was recognized, apprehended, and with the rest of his group ignominiously forced to return to Paris. Pathetically little remained of royal majesty. When he fled Louis had left behind him a document disavowing all the concessions he had made while under constraint. There was popular agitation for his deposition but, with some bloodshed in the open space of the Champ de Mars, this was suppressed and the royal office was tolerated for another year.

It was a critical year. During the summer, the constitution was completed, and the king signed it on the fourteenth of September. That document was, according to one contemporary, "a veritable monster: there was too much republic for a monarchy, and too much monarchy for a republic. The king was an *hors d'oeuvre*." The Constituent Assembly that had helped destroy an ancient order and give birth to a free society was dissolved and replaced by the Legislative Assembly, made up of entirely new members. Within six months this body, anticipating an attack upon France by Prussia and Austria, beat them to the draw by declaring war. Robespierre, a member of the old Assembly and one of the leading figures of the Revolution, had feared such a war. "We should be betrayed, thus defeated," he said. "Or else, were we to be the victors, the triumphant general would become the new enemy of the people."

With two very brief respites in 1802–03 and 1814–15, the war between revolutionary France and coalitions of European monarchies was to last for twenty-three years. Within a few months it led to the final downfall of the French monarchy, to the Reign of Terror, and to the complete disruption of the social fabric. War forced the revolutionists to face the stark alternative of victory against a formidable alliance or the destruction of their positive accomplishments—as well as their persons. And, justifying Robespierre's fears, it was the war which enabled Napoleon to demonstrate his military genius, to lead the Révolution to victory, to end the Revolution, and to substitute himself for it.

Napoleon was in Paris during the summer of 1792, straightening out the matter of his commission in the regular army and arranging for a leave to serve in the Corsican National Guard. (He was twenty-three years old.) On June 20, he and a friend were about to enter a restaurant near the Palais Royal when they saw a large mob armed with pikes, axes, swords, muskets, roasting spits, and sticks heading toward the Tuileries. They forewent dinner and followed the crowd, which, with thirteen thousand National Guards standing by, broke into the palace and confronted the king. They offered Louis two cockades—the white one of the old regime and of the armies forming in Germany, and the red, white, and blue one of the Revolution. Louis calmly chose the tricolor and placed the red bonnet of liberty on his head. His satisfied visitors offered him a drink of wine, which he took in hand, and remained in the palace four hours. Napoleon was appalled by the king's pusillanimity. Had *he* been king, he reflected, he would have ordered his troops to fire at the *canaille*—and disperse them with one volley.

Less than two months later, on August 10, 1792, Napoleon witnessed the overthrow of the monarchy. This time another mob, led by contingents of the National Guard just arrived from Marseilles

Louis XVI toasting the French Revolution with a liberty cup

Robespierre is shown executing the executioner, his last available victim.

(whose marching song, the *Marseillaise,* composed by Rouget de Lisle,
became the battle song of the Revolution, and later the national
anthem of France) invaded the Tuileries. The royal family found
asylum in the Legislative Assembly; when the king's Swiss Guards
opened fire in defense of the palace, Louis sent orders to them to cease,
whereupon those heroic defenders were massacred. Years later Napoleon recalled that no battlefield he had seen in his career gave the
impression of so many corpses as did the masses of dead Swiss on that
occasion. (At the time he wrote his brother that if Louis had appeared
on horseback he would have won the day.)

In September a National Convention was called to replace the Legislative Assembly, which had proved to be helpless, and it proceeded to
abolish the monarchy; Louis was tried for treason and condemned to
death; and on the twenty-first of January, 1793, he was guillotined on
the place de la Concorde (then called the place de la Révolution). Nine
months later Marie Antoinette, "a worn discrowned Widow of Thirty-
Eight, grey before her time," as Carlyle wrote, "was brought out . . .
bound, on a Cart" and decapitated in her turn.

The Republic was in serious trouble, threatened from without by
foreign enemies and from within by counterrevolutionary forces among
the clergy, the aristocrats, the peasants of the Vendée, and by moderates and opportunists of varied stripes. Acting as they felt it necessary
to save the Revolution from all its foes, within and without, the people
of Paris resorted to intimidation and to the most sanguinary violence.
Before the execution of the king, the government of Paris had been
taken over by an insurrectionary Commune that rounded up all those
suspected of counterrevolutionary activities or intentions and threw
them in jail, establishing a Revolutionary Tribunal to administer sum-
mary justice. In September, 1792, the bulging prisons were emptied
and all their inmates massacred, common criminals along with the rest.
It was the beginning of a blood bath that would drench all of France—
the Reign of Terror.

Virtually no one was safe from suspicion and slaughter. Murder became a demonstration of patriotism and an instrument of politics. At
Lyons the condemned were blown from the mouths of cannons; at
Angers, they were shot down to the sound of music; at Nantes victims
were drowned by the bargeful. Elsewhere the guillotine became almost

a diabolical machine of perpetual motion, to the point where a contemporary print represented Robespierre, having executed all others, guillotining the executioner. Actually, Robespierre himself was guillotined on July 28, 1794, in one of the culminating acts of the Terror.

The intensity of the Terror eased as the danger from the foreign enemy diminished. At the start of hostilities France was in chaos and its army disorganized. As they entered France, proceeding at the stately pace of eighteenth-century warfare, the allies confidently expected to arrive at Paris within a few weeks and to restore order to the grievously unsettled country; but France retaliated with a new concept of warfare. Until then European armies had been relatively small, officered by men of noble birth and made up in large part of professionals serving for pay and peasant recruits. The lesson of the American War of Independence had not yet been learned outside France. In spite of the emigration France still had the core of an excellent regular army, soon joined by volunteer units that quickly rose to its own level of efficiency. Then, on August 23, 1793, the Convention ordered a *levée en masse*—the total mobilization of the country. "Young men will go to the front," read the decree; "married men will forge arms and transport foodstuffs; women will make tents and uniforms and serve in the hospitals; children will tear rags into lint."

No less than fourteen armies (about a million and a half men) were thus raised and equipped within two years. These were the first European soldiers in more than a century who could regard the cause for which they were fighting as their own, the first ordinary men who were allowed to distinguish themselves individually by such acts of personal initiative and heroism as until then had been tolerated only in the wellborn. "Nothing equals the [French] soldiers' courage unless it is the cheerfulness with which they bear up under the most exhausting marches," Napoleon, then on active service, reported to his government at one point. "They sing in turn of fatherland and of love. . . . Everybody tells of what he has done, or else he talks about the next day's plan of operations, and often I find that they grasp things very clearly." In any case, by the end of 1793 the allies had been driven from France; in 1794 the French armies occupied the Low Countries and forged across the Rhine into Germany. In three years the republican armies had achieved what Louis XIV had been unable to accomplish in

almost fifty—control of the Channel coast and the middle and lower Rhine. By 1795 only England, Austria, and Sardinia, of the countries that had joined the coalition against France, remained in the field.

The success of republican arms added fuel to revolutionary ardor. To build a new society the dust of the past must be swept away. French history would begin again with a clean slate. In the autumn of 1793 the National Convention instituted a new calendar to start retroactively from September 22, 1792, a day that happily coincided with both the creation of the Republic and the autumnal equinox. Official acts would henceforth be dated from the year I of the Republic. The nomenclature of the new calendar would more closely correspond to the spirit and ideas of the times than the old Gregorian calendar. Names of days, months, and other intervals of time denoting a "natural" order of things replaced those with old religious associations. Thus, days of the week became Billy Goat, Plow, and Spinach; holidays were named

Volunteer recruits of the French Republican army, 1792

Opinion, Labor, and so forth; the months were to be known as Vende-maire (month of vintage), Thermidor (month of heat), Fructidor (month of fruit).

The Republican Calendar, the Convention solemnly declared, would be "a measure of time freed from all the errors which credulity and superstitious routine have handed down to us from centuries of ignor-ance." Sundays and the festival days of the Church were incompatible with this new chronology. From the start the Revolution had been, in effect, a new religion—a secular faith that, in the name of Reason, led to unreasonable violence toward the Church. On November 10, 1793, a great Festival of Reason was held in the cathedral of Notre Dame in Paris, presided over by an actress of the opera garbed in the dress of Liberty and posing as the Goddess of Reason. Thereafter most of the churches in France were either closed down or converted into Temples of Reason; often enough they were despoiled. By order of the Paris Commune a mob pulled down the ninety statues of the kings of Judah and Israel from the facade of Notre Dame, mistaking them for figures of the kings of France. Starting in 1793 the celebrated abbey church at Cluny, that had for so long been one of Christendom's most splendid monuments, was gradually demolished. The sculptures of the church of Saint-Denis were also removed, and the actual remains of the kings of France who had been buried there were dug up and thrown into a common ditch. Nothing was held inviolable. The embalmed hearts of Louis XIII and XIV were removed from repositories in the church of Saint-Paul, pulverized, and added to the pigments of some strong-stomached painter. At Chartres the great cathedral was spared total demolition only because one architect pointed out that its debris would completely block the streets. Every reminder of ancient despot-ism, chateaux along with religious buildings, was threatened with mutilation or destruction. "In the space of three days," Chateaubriand lamented, "men destroyed the achievements of twelve centuries." This was done deliberately, by order of public authorities, and paid for at fixed rates according to the magnitude or difficulty of the job involved.

The *coup d'état* of 9 Thermidor (July 27, 1794) that sent Robes-pierre to the guillotine not only ended the Reign of Terror but con-cluded the radical phase of the Revolution. It initiated what is called the Thermidorean reaction, a period in which those who had survived the slaughter and the political upheavals tried to consolidate their positions of power. However, the new regime, born of a *coup d'état,* was to live by *coups d'état* and finally to die by a *coup d'état.* In 1795 another constitution (the third since 1789) was framed and a new government, called the Directory, replaced the outgoing Convention. There followed more than four years of incompetence, corruption, intrigue, bankruptcy—and continued wars. The French people wanted peace, but the government was financed by tribute money exacted by its victorious armies from conquered lands.

One of the accomplishments of the Revolution had been to open the door to leadership in the army to men of other than noble origin. (The principle had been established under the monarchy, but the practical results came under the Republic.) Among the brightest of such rising stars was the young Corsican Napoleon Bonaparte, who had been promoted from captain to brigadier general in 1793 after he played a critical part in dislodging the English and royalist forces from Toulon. (He virtually stumbled on that scene of action after having been forced to flee Corsica for political reasons.) Two years later, he attracted greater attention by dispersing—with a "whiff of grapeshot," as he reported—counterrevolutionary forces in Paris that seriously threatened to unseat the Directory; he thereby earned the approval and confidence of that body. Soon after, he was given command of the Army of Italy, which had been stalled at the foot of the Alps for several years, with instructions to drive out the Austrian troops deployed in Piedmont and Lombardy. Napoleon now stepped boldly onto the world stage.

Napoleon's exploits in that first major campaign of his career were formidable and rocketed him to fame. This twenty-six-year-old general, who stood 5 feet 2 inches tall and whose most decisive feat of arms had been the massacre of a few hundred civilians in the rue Saint-Honoré during the insurrection a year earlier, took over a demoralized army in bad physical condition and forged it into a keen, highly tempered instrument of war. He started this great adventure with an electrifying proclamation to his troops: "Soldiers! You are ill-fed and almost naked. The government owes you a great deal, but it can do nothing for you. Your patience and courage do you honor but give you neither worldly goods nor glory. I shall lead you into the most fertile plains on earth. There you will find great cities and rich provinces. There you will

FLANDRE
Lille
ARTOIS
Arras
Amiens
PICARDY
Rouen
ILE DE FRANCE
Caen
NORMANDY
Paris
LORRAINE
Nancy
Strasbourg
CHAMPAGNE
ALSACE
BRITTANY
Rennes
MAINE
Le Mans
Orleans
ORLEANAIS
Troyes
Dijon
Besancon
ANJOU
Angers
Tours
NIEVRE
FRANCHE-COMTE
Nantes
TOURAINE
BERRY
Bourges
Nevers
POITOU
Poitou
BURGUNDY
La Rochelle
Gueret
Moulins
AUNIS
SAINTONGE
MARCHE
BOURBONNAIS
Saintes
ANGOUMOIS
Limoges
LYONNAIS
Lyons
SAVOY
Angouleme
LIMOUSIN
Clermont-Ferrand
Chambery
Bordeaux
AUVERGNE
Grenoble
DAUPHINE
GUYENNE & GASCONY
COMTAT
VENAISSIN
COMTE
DE NICE
Avignon
PROVENCE
Nice
Bayonne
LANGUEDOC
Aix
NAVARRE
Pau
Toulouse
Marseilles
BEARN
COMTE
DE FOIX
Foix
Perpignan
ROUSSILLON

find honor, glory, riches. Soldiers of the Army of Italy! Could courage and constancy possibly fail you?" It was true that, unlike the troops opposing them, the French had a personal stake in victory. Defeat meant to them starvation, rags, and misery; victory meant food, cash, clothes, women, and wine. And they conquered—at Lodi, Milan, Arcole, Rivoli, and elsewhere. Soon the French soldiers were being paid in hard money and could appear at La Scala, on the Corso, in the cafés and drawing rooms, in becoming attire. (For a while, at least, they were received at such places with enthusiasm.) In their wake came French art commissioners who systematically looted the art treasures of Italy and sent them back to the Louvre, recently established as a national museum (for a while it would be called the Musée Napoléon). The treasury of the Directory was temporarily replenished. When he returned to France Napoleon was the idol of half of Europe.

His next adventure, the expedition to Egypt, was planned as a bold attack on the British Empire by conquering the Near East, but it ended in disaster. Napoleon's brilliant victory over the Mamelukes at the battle of the Pyramids in July, 1798, was nullified when Lord Nelson destroyed the French fleet at Aboukir. Matters worsened when plague broke out in the French army. As difficulties mounted, Napoleon, learning that at home both the Directory and its European armies were in serious trouble, quit his troops in Egypt, leaving them in a hopeless situation, and returned to France (preceded by the report of his latest "victory"), where he was hailed as the man of the hour. With the country in political and financial crisis, the fruit was ripe for the returning hero to pick.

The period that followed, up until the climactic encounter at Waterloo in 1815, has ever since been known as the age of Napoleon. During those crucial years the "little Corsican" played such a dominant role in the shaping of European history that, as has been said, the man quickly became the epoch. As early as 1790 Edmund Burke had quite accurately predicted that the French Revolution would end in a military dictatorship. Very soon after Napoleon's return from Egypt that prophecy was fulfilled. On November 9, 1799, the Directory was overthrown in favor of a Consulate with Napoleon as first consul; he promptly moved into the Luxembourg Palace and assumed complete control of the nation. His administration was skillful and vigorous.

A map outlining the historical regions of France

Within three years he reformed the country's finances and its legal structure, arranged a peace with the Church, and brought the war against France's enemies to a successful if temporary conclusion. With the peace of Amiens, signed in 1802, France became once again the supreme power on the Continent. Two years later, on December 2, 1804, in the cathedral of Notre Dame at Paris, Napoleon took the imperial crown from the hands of Pope Pius VII, whom he had summoned from Rome, and placed it on his own head. (According to one account, Napoleon yawned during the proceedings.)

Up until the final turning point of his fortune, the saga of Napoleon's career is the greatest success story ever told. Probably no other mortal has received so much attention from biographers and historians, critics and enthusiasts; the career of no other historical figure has been studied in more exhaustive detail. There is little need to trace the successive triumphs that followed his self-coronation. Another coalition had formed against France, but the Austrians were crushed at Ulm, the combined Russians and Austrians at Austerlitz, Prussia at Jena, and the Russians again at Eylau. Then Sweden capitulated, leaving only England to deal with. More than a thousand years after Pope Leo had crowned Charlemagne in Saint Peter's, almost two thousand years after Caesar had conquered Pompey at Pharsalia, Napoleon Bonaparte, self-styled "emperor of the French," had overcome the emperors of Austria and Russia, who claimed to represent the old and the new Rome respectively; and at the peak of his influence, his international domain included a greater area than the European holdings of either Charlemagne or Caesar. Within a year and a half he created more kings than the Holy Roman Emperors had in a millennium, most of them from the ranks of his own family, whom he settled on the thrones of kingdoms he had conquered. "One of these days," his mother reflected philosophically, "I shall have seven or eight sovereigns on my hands."

Napoleon was greatly impressed by the art of Jacques Louis David, a painter who he thought could persuasively represent him as a modern counterpart of the great empire builders of ancient Rome. David had already had an extraordinary career. He began as a protégé of the state under the *ancien régime;* he continued as the artist of the Revolution—and a political figure to boot; and he then became first court painter to the emperor, whose commissions obliged the artist to employ so many

Jacques Louis David's drawing of Napoleon crowning himself emperor

assistants that his shop amounted to an official school of art. In that atelier was painted the largest of David's tributes to Napoleon, in which he portrayed his patron, already wearing the wreath of a Roman emperor, about to crown his wife Josephine. David's efforts to recreate in his paintings the ancient world as he imagined it had a pervasive influence on fashion and decoration. The neoclassical furniture and other forms he had had constructed from his own designs for his compositions and for use in his studios were widely copied. They became common carriers of the "Empire" style that spread everywhere in Europe in the wake of Napoleon's victories.

As part of the plan to glorify his reign and to celebrate his victories Napoleon hoped to make Paris not only "the most beautiful city there is, and the most beautiful city there ever was, but also the most beautiful city there ever could be." Fortunately, the cathedral of Notre Dame, scheduled for demolition in the heated days of the Revolution and for a time used as a storage place for wine, had been spared. Following Napoleon's concordat with the pope in 1801 the cathedral once again became a Roman Catholic place of worship. As consul, Napoleon completed the east court of the Louvre (the Cour Carrée) that had been left unfinished since the time of Louis XIV. At the other end of that great complex he had raised a monumental arch, the Arc de Triomphe du Carrousel so familiar to today's tourists, to commemorate his triumphant campaigns of 1805. Along the northern side of the Louvre the rue de Rivoli was designed to celebrate the victory of his Italian campaign years before. In the place Vendôme a great column was raised, in imitation of Trajan's column in Rome, surmounted by a statue of Napoleon garbed as Caesar. It was sheathed in the bronze recast from cannons that had been captured from the Austrians and Russians at Austerlitz (and stands today over an underground garage opposite the Ritz). Another great triumphal arch was planned at the western end of the Champs-Élysées, at the place de l'Étoile, but it was not finished for years to come. New bridges were put up across the Seine—the Pont des Arts, the Pont d'Austerlitz, the Pont d'Iéna, among others; fourteen of them spanned the river in barely more than a mile at the heart of Paris.

Napoleon's rise to absolute power had been an almost inevitable consequence of the Reign of Terror, which had imbued Frenchmen

Ossian welcoming the generals of Napoleon's army to Valhalla

with such a mutual hatred as only despotism could control. Beyond that, even those who deplored the Terror preferred it to seeing France invaded by foreign armies. After Thermidor the corruption and instability of civilian authorities led the armies of France to give their primary allegiance to their victorious leaders. In a sense the troops became the nation; they preserved the spirit of the Revolution in its purity; and Napoleon, their supreme commander, became the hope of France.

Napoleon had had nothing to do with the convulsive beginnings of the Revolution, but when he assumed power in France he appeared to many to be "the Revolution incarnate," as Metternich termed him—the embodiment of its spirit and the savior of its principles. It is true that wherever Napoleon forced his way abroad he introduced the ideas and in some measure the achievements of the French Revolution. Goethe stated with more enthusiasm than accuracy that Napoleon was the expression of all that was reasonable, legitimate, and European in the revolutionary movement. And there were others, Beethoven among them, who applauded his performance in this respect—until the oppressively high price of "liberation" was made clear. At home he consolidated and refined what had for the most part already been accomplished. Even during the Reign of Terror it was painfully evident that the laws initiated by the Revolution had to be reconciled with what remained of the customary laws of the land. This was done under Napoleon's direction with the Civil Code, or *Code Napoléon,* generally regarded as his most solid and lasting accomplishment. With that and attendant legal reforms, he maintained he had given permanence to the essential contributions of the Revolution—national unity and civic equality. That code, Napoleon claimed, was "the code of the age. It not only ordains tolerance but systematizes it, and tolerance is the greatest blessing of mankind." Others have deemed it one of the few books that have influenced the whole world. It remains (modified and amended) the basis of civil law in large areas of the modern world, even in polities where common law generally prevails—as in Louisiana in the United States and in Quebec in the British Commonwealth.

By his own confession Napoleon's ultimate objectives were not always clear to himself. In the last analysis it was his destiny that seemed to matter most. "All my life," he wrote, "I have sacrificed everything—comfort, self-interest, happiness—to my destiny." Exalted by his successes, he identified or confused that destiny with the destiny of civilization itself. As Mme de Staël observed, "he wanted to put his gigantic self in the place of mankind."

Eventually he ran out of successes. As early as 1805 Lord Nelson's naval victory at Cape Trafalgar over a Franco-Spanish fleet put an end to Napoleon's grandiose plan to invade England. "England expects that every man will do his duty," Nelson signaled his fleet before he was killed in the conflict. The ensuing action resulted in the most glorious victory in the history of the English navy. Three years later, the Peninsular War brought further frustration. "I admit that I started off on the wrong foot in this whole [Spanish] business . . . ," Napoleon recalled. "The whole thing remains ugly, since I lost out. . . ." The disastrous Russian campaign of the winter of 1812, however, was the real beginning of Napoleon's end. He had assembled an army of nearly 600,000 men, the largest military force under one command that Europe had ever seen. He lost more than half that number as casualties during the winter. His forced retreat from Moscow was an almost indescribable epic of horror.

Even with that frightful reverse Napoleon continued to fight in other sectors. He could not yet believe that defeat was to be his ultimate destiny. But on March 31, 1814, the allied armies that were opposing him entered Paris. Napoleon abdicated and left for exile in Elba. His return to France and the "Hundred Days" that followed, ending in his defeat at Waterloo, was an anticlimax—an epilogue to a story that was already finished.

Looking back from his final exile at Saint Helena Napoleon chose to believe that in the end his defeat had been beyond the reach of either man or reason; he was overpowered by the very elements. "In the south it was the sea that destroyed me; and in the north it was the fire of Moscow and the ice of winter; so there it is, water, air, fire, all nature and nothing but nature; these were the opponents of a universal regeneration commanded by Nature herself! The problems of Nature are insoluble!" In such a spirit of rationalization he began the creation of a Napoleonic legend that grew luxuriantly in years to come.

CHAPTER VIII

RESTORATIONS
OF ROYALTY

While Napoleon withdrew from the scene an international congress assembled at Vienna to reorganize Europe after the shattering experiences of the past twenty-five years. At that point, in 1814, the situation was contrary to just about everything Napoleon had hoped and fought for. After all their heroic and wide-ranging campaigns, from the Nile to Moscow, his armies had finally been beaten back within the "natural" frontiers of France. When peace was established England stood firmly at the crossroads of world commerce, undisputed mistress of the seas. Russia had emerged, stronger than ever, as an important power in western Europe. A way had been prepared for a federation of German states under the domination of Prussia. The people of Italy, a land so often dismembered by foreign invaders and divided by local circumstances, had been reminded of their ancient unity. France faced the aroused nationalism of neighboring countries that were determined to prevent her ever again from breaking out from her borders and attempting to impose her will on the rest of the Continent.

Actually, the terms of the peace imposed upon France were not unduly harsh, even though they were made somewhat more severe

A massacre in a Paris street during the uprisings of 1848

after Napoleon's return from Elba and his desperate adventure at Waterloo. Thereupon the French borders were reduced somewhat within their limits of 1789 (for strategic reasons the Saar was one of the areas taken from France; its economic importance was not yet imagined); the country was subjected to an indemnity, and until such reparation was made an allied army of occupation was to remain on French soil. However, that indemnity was paid in full within three years and the allied troops were withdrawn. Meanwhile, as part of the final settlement, most of the art treasures Napoleon's armies and emissaries had looted from other European countries were returned. Among other items, the great bronze horses were removed from Napoleon's Arch of the Carousel and reinstalled on Saint Mark's in Venice.

Thanks to shrewd negotiations by Talleyrand, the allied victors agreed to restore the Bourbons to the French throne in the person of the late king's younger brother, who returned from his years of exile as Louis XVIII a few weeks after Napoleon's flight to Elba. When, with the news of Napoleon's abdication, this last of the Louis' had been told that he was now king of France, he had rejoined, "Have I ever ceased to be?" Upon his return he claimed to be king of France and Navarre "by the grace of God," and he brought in his train émigré courtiers, headed by his brother Charles, count of Artois, who had "learned nothing and forgotten nothing" in the years since 1789.

However, a constitutional charter was hastily drawn up and "granted" by Louis to the nation. Freedom of religion and of the press was promised along with other basic rights the people had gained after the overthrow of the *ancien régime*. The administrative organization of the state prescribed by Napoleon was left untouched. That system has been described as "the most powerful instrument of bureaucratic control that the Western world had known since the Roman Empire." With this alone, Napoleon had left an impress on France that was more important and more enduring than anything accomplished by the Sun King in all his glory.

The new regime got off to an uncertain start. When news of Napoleon's return from Elba was announced, no one rose to the defense of the Bourbons, and Louis, with his court, hastily fled across the border. After Waterloo he returned "in the baggage train of the allied armies." Yet, in spite of his ignominious retreat and his inglorious return, Louis

was accepted a second time by his people—and not without enthusiasm
—for France was weary of war and bloodshed. Louis, too, wanted a quiet, peaceful reign. Grotesquely obese, gouty, and, almost sixty, wearied by the adversities of his years of exile, he was not a dynamic ruler. What followed seemed in some ways like a dreary anticlimax after the world-shaking happenings—the prodigious undertakings, the heroic sacrifices, the bloody tragedies—of the past quarter century. France and all Europe suffered the *mal du siècle,* the "illness of the century," which spread in epidemic fashion among the romantics whose soulful strivings were creating new worlds of art and literature and philosophy as the century advanced. As a matter of somewhat puzzling fact, one of the dullest periods in French politics and of French life coincided with an exceptionally brilliant flowering by French culture.

The political and domestic currents of the Restoration can be quickly charted. Louis attempted to institute a moderate program, hoping to reconcile the liberals, who wished to strengthen parliamentary institutions, and the conservatives, headed by his brother Charles and dubbed the "ultraroyalists," or simply "ultras," who wished to re-establish an absolute monarchy. As the king grew older and more infirm, the latter group gained in influence and, when Louis died in 1824 and his brother succeeded him as Charles X, took command of the French government.

Charles was crowned at Reims with pomp and ceremony that recalled the coronations of the *ancien régime.* He proclaimed his intention of ruling by divine right as the Most Christian King of France, and it was soon apparent that he had no intentions of playing the part of a constitutional monarch. "I would rather hew wood," he exclaimed at one point, "than be a king under the conditions of the king of England." His acts as well as his pronouncements led to the king's growing unpopularity. He generously compensated his émigré supporters for lands that had been confiscated during the Revolution; other measures put increased power into the hands of the Jesuits and ultramontanes (the supporters of papal policy in political and ecclesiastical matters), to the dismay of Gallicans (those who favored restrictions of papal control and national autonomy in such matters) and liberals alike. (Wellington observed that Charles "was setting up a government by priests, through priests, for priests.") Growing opposition to his program served only to make Charles more obstinate. Divine right could make no compromises with the will of the people. On July 25, 1830, upon advice from his ministers, he virtually suspended the constitution. The next day he spent hunting, as his brother Louis XVI had done in generally similar circumstances so many years before; he had indeed "learned nothing and forgotten nothing" in the long interim. Now barricades were thrown up in the streets of Paris. Workingmen and shopkeepers joined with artists, students, journalists, veterans of Napoleon's wars, and still others in mounting a revolution. After three bloody days of street fighting—*les trois glorieuses,* so dramatically memorialized by Delacroix's painting "Liberty Leading the People"— the restored Bourbon monarchy was overthrown.

It has been said that if Charles X did not know how to rule, he knew how to cease to rule. Accompanied by an escort of twelve hundred men, he proceeded to Cherbourg with stately dignity and, dismissing his entourage, embarked with his family from there for England. Thus, almost ceremoniously, the last of the Bourbons left the throne of France. No effort was made either to stop him or to bring him back. The French people were happy to be rid of him; his aristocratic supporters and counsellors offered no resistance at all to his overthrow and simply retired from public life. Once again, as in 1792, republicans wished to abolish the monarchy altogether; once again the moderates prevailed; and once again Lafayette, the aging and perennial moderate, in 1830 as in 1792, helped precipitate matters by championing Louis Philippe, the duke of Orléans, to occupy the vacant throne.

Both Lafayette and Louis Philippe had served with the French forces as general officers during the early years of the Revolution; both had quit their commands in the field in disagreement with extremist policies of the National Convention, and had fled the country. Lafayette was imprisoned for five years in Austria before his release was secured by Napoleon. Louis Philippe found his way to America where, following an itinerary suggested by George Washington, he made a tour of the western parts of the new nation. In 1830 Lafayette, now seventy-three, had recently made a triumphal return visit to the United States that had greatly enhanced his prestige. He assured his countrymen that Louis Philippe would prove worthy of their trust, and his persuasion was important in the making of the new king.

A detail of Delacroix's painting "Liberty Leading the People" during the July revolution of 1830

France was not yet ready for another republic. The French people had once again demonstrated how they could make royalty capitulate, and once again they chose monarchy as their form of government. In any case, the institution of another republic would have renewed the hostility of all Europe. With Louis Philippe France hoped to have the best of both worlds. He was "a prince devoted to the principles of the Revolution" and had "carried the tricolor under fire"; he would be a "citizen king." He was proclaimed "king of the French," not king of France, and king not only by the grace of God but also "by the will of the people."

Louis Philippe's reign, called the July Monarchy, lasted for eighteen years. The new king was one of the richest men in France and his rule was a frank plutocracy. Less than a quarter of a million Frenchmen,

Honoré Daumier's lithograph "Murder in the rue Transnonain," 1834

men of some property, had the right to vote; those who wanted the franchise were baldly advised to "get rich." Membership in the National Guard was limited to citizens who paid direct taxes and bought their own uniforms ("grocer janissaries," as they were called by critics of the system). The bourgeoisie, that had so long been struggling for authority, was officially enthroned at last.

Louis Philippe started off by playing his part as citizen king and a true bourgeois among the bourgeois. He strolled about the streets of Paris unattended, carrying an umbrella rather than a sword or any other symbol of rank. He guarded his personal fortune and drove hard bargains with his bourgeois parlement. Karl Marx described the regime as a "company for the exploitation of French national wealth," with Louis Philippe as director and with his ministers, deputies, and the limited number of voters as shareholders who could claim their dividends. Among those who were not qualified for such preferential consideration—the petite bourgeoisie, the proletariat, the small landholders, along with those who wanted their ruler to cut a more regal figure, the Citizen King (he was also called the Grocer King) was not popular. He was mercilessly caricatured in the free press and repeated attempts were made on his life. (He once bitterly remarked that on him alone there was no closed hunting season.) There were frequent uprisings in the streets of French cities. In 1834, in a house on the rue Transnonain in Paris, innocent people were mercilessly butchered by troops detailed to crush a republican outburst. The tragic incident, one of a number of violent episodes in those years of trouble, may have been all but forgotten had not Honoré Daumier immortalized it in a lithograph of unforgettable poignancy.

There were still others who wanted France to be more aggressive in foreign affairs, who deplored the pacifism that, among other things, led the king into an *entente cordiale* with Great Britain at a time when the French public was distinctly anglophobic. In 1843 Queen Victoria paid a state visit to Louis Philippe and found the French court both disorganized and undignified. In one significant area, however, in Algeria, France acted militantly. The conquest of Algeria had been undertaken during the last days of Charles X, and Louis Philippe carried it to a conclusion. It was the one colorful adventure of the drab, homespun July Monarchy. It took eighteen years and many thousands of

160 French troops to overcome the opposition they encountered from Arab and Berber tribesmen in the rocky fastnesses of that land; and those victories entailed consequences that would be painfully felt more than a century later.

Such distant triumphs, even on those exotic battlegrounds, were not enough to compensate the French public for the dullness of national life. As the poet Lamartine observed, "France was bored." It was under such circumstances that the legend of Napoleon, which he himself had nurtured until his death at Saint Helena in 1821, came to full flower. Years before, in 1800, the little Corsican had written to one of his generals: "Greatness has its beauties, but only in retrospect and in the imagination." To the romantic heirs of his epic age, to a generation starved for glory, Napoleon became in retrospect a symbol of human genius struggling with Fate—a Prometheus reborn to fire the insatiable yearnings of the human spirit.

Completely lacking in any such heroic qualities, peace-loving, and uninspired, Louis Philippe did what he could to revive memories of the grandeur of the Empire and the greatness of Napoleon. In 1814 the statue of the emperor, represented as Caesar, had been removed from atop the column in the place Vendôme; now another figure of Napoleon, as the Little Corporal this time, was put in that place. On October 25, 1836, the royal family and more than two hundred thousand spectators celebrated the erection of a huge obelisk, a gift from the viceroy of Egypt, in the place de la Concorde—a monument that inevitably recalled the Egyptian campaigns of Napoleon. The colossal Arc de Triomphe in the Étoile (renamed place Charles de Gaulle in 1970) that had been planned to celebrate the victories of Napoleon and of the Revolution, but that remained unfinished for twenty years, was completed the same year. Fourteen years later, the Citizen King had the emperor's remains brought back to France and laid to rest in the chapel of the Invalides in Paris, thus honoring the emperor's last wish that he be buried "on the banks of the Seine, amidst the French people I loved so well."

Drawn by sixteen horses and surrounded by old veterans "bronzed with the sun of the Pyramids, stiff with the ice of the Berezina," a magnificent catafalque bore Napoleon's coffin beneath the great arch and down the Champs-Élysées. As the procession passed the masses of

A detail of the "Marseillaise" from the Arc de Triomphe, Paris

people who lined the way, for the first time in a quarter of a century the old shout could be heard: *Vive l'Empereur!* Thus "by the voice of national memory, rising ghostlike in the chill winter air, the dead emperor was raised to immortality." In view of events to come that shout should have filled Louis Philippe with misgivings over his imprudence in making such a splendid melodramatic gesture.

The same year, in 1840, Victor Hugo, the son of one of Napoleon's generals, was elected to the French Academy. Thanks to the influence of the king's daughter-in-law, he not only won this distinction at a relatively young age, but he also became a peer of France—and he never forgot his indebtedness to the house of Orléans in his long and very illustrious career. The year of Louis Philippe's enthronement, in 1830, Hugo had staged his poetic drama *Hernani,* a play so insurgent in style and content that it caused nightly near-riots at the Comédie Française. That year also the *Symphonie Fantastique* of Hector Berlioz had its first performance, a work of such strange and rich orchestration as had never before been heard, a witches' sabbath described with what seemed to many a delirium of sound.

With their startling accomplishments these young men (they were both still in their twenties) became the standard-bearers of the romantic movement that was sweeping in a rising tide across the Western world as the nineteenth century advanced. A generation earlier that tide had grown with the works of Chateaubriand, Mme de Staël, and André Chénier. Now small armies of young writers, artists, and students brought fresh talent and imagination to new, revolutionary forms of expression. "There exists today," Hugo asserted in defense of his work, "a literary old regime, as there once existed a political old regime." He and his advanced contemporaries were determined to topple the old and establish the new. As Théophile Gautier recalled in describing the mixed audience that had attended the performance of *Hernani,* "two systems, two parties, two armies, two civilizations—it is no exaggeration to put it so—were facing each other, filled with cordial reciprocal hatred. . . ." And the long-haired youth with their "peculiar costumes and fierce looks," the romantics, were to win the day.

With his paintings Eugène Delacroix became a symbol of liberation and revolution in the arts. He was obsessed by the expressive power of pigment, and the audacity with which he juxtaposed broad strokes of primary colors led his detractors to ridicule him for using a "drunken broom" for a brush. Even his friends found it difficult to accept the "confused" composition, the "unfinished" drawing, the unrestrained opulence of such canvases as the "Massacre at Chios" (it was dubbed the "massacre of painting"). But with massive will he pursued his personal vision to heights approached by none of his romantic contemporaries in painting. The intelligence, urbanity, and integrity that made Delacroix a revolutionary in his studio endeared him as a person to the most cultivated and progressive minds of his day. Baudelaire, Gautier, Balzac, Dumas *père,* Chopin, and George Sand were among those who welcomed him to their conversational circles.

While these men and women with many others in France and elsewhere in Europe were carrying the romantic movement to climactic developments, inaugurating a new era of artistic and literary freedom that twentieth-century modernism would push to its logical conclusion, public life under the July Monarchy continued in prosaic fashion. The political system of the bourgeois regime was too comfortably established to respond to the changes that were taking place in French life and thought during the 1830s and 1840s. In his great collection of novels and short stories which he entitled *The Human Comedy,* Honoré de Balzac drew a detailed, realistic picture of daily social experience during those years, with a cast of more than two thousand individual characters to document his narratives.

All France files through those pages. Beneath the surface of the life there so intimately described, eruptive forces were gathering. Corruption in government circles had become an open scandal. The proletariat was writhing under the inequities of its lot, which had become more pronounced with the Industrial Revolution. A demand for wider suffrage became insistent. Paris had become the international headquarters for various radical movements from which modern socialist theory emerged. In 1846 a bad harvest and a potato blight that affected most of western Europe coincided with an industrial crisis that threw large numbers of people out of work. Agitation for reforms increased.

It had become obvious that the apparent stability of the government was rather a form of paralysis. In February, 1848, a procession of protest coursed through the streets of Paris. The National Guard was summoned to defend the king (who had not reviewed that organization

Eugeǹe Delacroix's romantic painting of "The Abduction of Rebecca"

for eight years); its members assembled unwillingly, shouting *Vive la Reforme!* and singing the *Marseillaise*. A day later crowds that Victor Hugo observed singing cheerfully as they roamed the boulevards were met at one point by a volley of gunfire from regular troops, under circumstances that are not altogether clear. Whether it was a mistake or an accident hardly mattered. That fusillade turned a popular demonstration into a revolution. "The bodies of the victims were loaded on a cart lit with torches," wrote Hugo. "The cortege moved back amidst curses at a funeral pace." And in a few hours the streets of Paris were blocked with barricades. The city was in the hands of the mob, which advanced toward the Tuileries. On the twenty-fourth of February, Louis Philippe abdicated and fled Paris in a cab, finally reaching England under the thoroughly bourgeois name of Mr. Smith. The last descendant of Hugh Capet had quit the throne of France.

Louis Philippe had abdicated in favor of his grandson, the count of Paris, but instead a provisional government hastily formed to meet the emergency and, under riotous pressure from the Paris mob, for the second time in French history abolished the monarchy and established a republic. Immediately quarrels broke out between the right and left wings of the new government, the latter strongly re-enforced by support from the city's mobs. In the spring of 1848, however, elections were held to the National Assembly, which was to give France a new constitution, and the right wing—the moderate republicans—won a substantial victory at the polls. For the first time the elections were based on universal manhood suffrage, which, among other things, gave the provinces an authority that earlier had been largely limited to Paris.

With the extension of the franchise the millions of mostly illiterate peasants, long thought of as potential revolutionaries, proved to be more conservative than the qualified voters of past years. But the laboring masses of Paris, their ranks swollen by migrants from the countryside who had left their blighted farms to search for gainful employment in the city, clamored for relief. A public works program had been established to alleviate their distress, but it turned into a system for paying the unemployed a miserable dole. Protests grew into violence.

In May the disgruntled workers actually overturned the government for a brief spell, long enough to terrify the conservative guardians of law and order with the specter of a "red" uprising. The workmen enrolled in the relief program, more than one hundred thousand strong by June, were denounced as "pretorians of revolt." Alexis de Tocqueville, a member of the Assembly who some years before had written a profound study, *Democracy in America,* later recalled that he found in Paris "a hundred thousand armed workingmen formed into regiments dying with hunger, but their minds filled with vain theories and visionary hopes." He wrote, "I saw Society cut in two: those who possessed nothing united in greed; those who possessed something united in common terror." Only a great battle fought in the streets of Paris, he averred with perfect hindsight, could end the crisis. On the twenty-first of June, the laborers were discharged from the national workshops (the relief rolls had placed an intolerable burden on the government's budget) and were told to find jobs outside Paris or to enlist in the army. That gave the signal for a furious insurrection. The following days Paris witnessed the bloodiest street fighting in the history of Europe. The workmen, as Tocqueville observed, had been issued weapons after the February revolution, and it took 30,000 troops and 16,000 guardsmen, advancing from street to street with the support of cannon, to restore order. When the massacre was over, the army held power in France and the Assembly managed to survive under its protection.

Viewing the chaos from across the Channel, the duke of Wellington wrote, "France needs a Napoleon! I cannot yet see him . . . Where is he?" The answer came soon enough. By November the Assembly had completed its proposals for a new constitution, and when elections were held the next month Louis Napoleon Bonaparte, nephew of the great emperor, was elected to the presidency of the Republic by an overwhelming majority. Twice in years past Louis Napoleon had vainly tried to excite the French into revolting against Louis Philippe. Following his second attempt, in 1840, he was confined in the small town of Ham in northern France (on the very day his uncle's remains were deposited at the Invalides) ; the "University of Ham," he called it, for while imprisoned he studied diligently, wrote various tracts on social and political subjects, corresponded with various influential persons, and collaborated with French journalists of the left.

In May, 1846, he escaped to England where he made up for his six years of isolation "by a furious pursuit of pleasure," and kept an attentive eye on developments in France. "They [the French people] will come to me without any effort of my own," he predicted. And so they did after the horrors of the June demonstrations. Dismayed by the implications of those insurrections, and beguiled by the legend of Napoleon I, the nation turned for leadership, almost reflexively, to another Bonaparte, to a name forever associated with order and system—and glory. "The name . . . is in itself a program," Louis Bonaparte remarked on one occasion; "it stands for order, authority, religion and the welfare of the people in internal affairs, and in foreign affairs for the national dignity."

Under the new constitution the president was elected for an unrenewable four-year term. Louis Bonaparte took the oath of loyalty to the Republic and swore allegiance to the constitution; and he kept his own counsel. While in exile he had written, "Today the reign of castes is finished; one cannot govern except by means of the masses . . . [which] must be organized so that they can formulate their will, and disciplined so that they can be directed and enlightened about their true interests." Of such thoughts modern totalitarianism was made; and, in fact, during his first years in office Louis shrewdly prepared the way for his assumption of dictatorial power. He conciliated the Catholic opposition by permitting a French army to restore Pope Pius IX to Rome (the pontiff had been forced to flee the city by Italian nationalists, who were angered by his refusal to support anti-Austrian rebels in 1848), and by sponsoring an education bill that favored the Church. He bore down on radicalism with increasing severity; he favored royalist sympathizers with positions in high office; and he strengthened his support from the military by enlarging the army.

In December, 1851, with these and other means, he was able to engineer a *coup d'état* that gave him dictatorial powers under a new constitution. Eleven months later he was acclaimed emperor of the French as Napoleon III (the son of Napoleon I, whom his father on abdication had named as successor, had died earlier). For the next seven years, as the new emperor practically paralyzed the legislature, the press, electoral procedures, and other forms of public expression, France had no political life.

Louis was then almost forty-five years old, somewhat portly, wearing a novel combination of mustache and goatee that was widely imitated—and had a roving eye. Looking for new worlds to conquer, early

OVERLEAF: *Winterhalter's painting of the Princess Eugénie and her ladies in waiting dressed in their crinolines*

in 1853 he married a Spanish beauty of noble birth, Eugénie Marie de Montijo de Guzmán, after discovering that he could have that "notorious virgin" only in wedlock. (She was the granddaughter of the United States consul at Málaga, who was a Scotsman by birth and an American by nationality.) Three years later she presented her husband with a son and heir, after which whatever romance there had been in the union seems to have vanished and the emperor returned to his mistresses. However, by her beauty, elegance, and charm Eugénie added special brilliance to the imperial court and regime. At the Tuileries, at Compiègne, and at Biarritz, which the empress helped make fashionable by her visits, Eugénie and the ladies of the court bared their handsome shoulders in low-necked crinoline gowns, and posed for their portraits by Franz Winterhalter, a famous painter of Second Empire society. (The papal nuncio once remarked that those wide skirts used so much material there was none left for the bodice.)

It was a period of great prosperity and of glittering social life. Of that social life the artist Constantin Guys left thousands of drawings, showing courtesans and gallants in the course of their daily rounds; the ladies in a froth of ribbons and stuffs parading along the Champs-Élysées or the avenue du bois de Boulogne, behind elegant coachmen in smart carriages drawn by sleek, high-stepping horses, as men of fashion and uniformed officers eye their progress. In his sketches also, women in brothels raise their skirts to dance with abandon, their bosoms slipping out of their deep décolletage. It was in 1855 that Alexandre Dumas *fils* added the word *demimonde* to the Parisian vocabulary, and in the years immediately following that Jacques Levy Offenbach, son of a Jewish cantor, composed the comic operas (including *La Vie Parisienne*) that gave Paris its reputation as a city of gay living and pleasure seeking. In Victorian England French novels were read surreptitiously to avoid scandal; and Englishmen escaped to France for pleasures not to be had at home. In 1869 the Folies Bergères was founded; the cancan was danced everywhere. When he first encountered the dance a few years later on a visit to France, Mark Twain wrote that he placed his hands before his face "for very shame." However, he admitted that he looked through his fingers and was astounded by what he saw.

Long before his *coup d'état,* it seems, Napoleon III had dreamed of

transforming Paris into the "capital of capitals," in continuation of the improvements that had been undertaken by his uncle. Napoleon I had built the Madeleine, the Bourse, and some other fine buildings, but his career was interrupted before he could rebuild Paris itself (as Voltaire had long before demanded). This, Louis Napoleon undertook as one of the first acts of his reign as emperor when, in June, 1853, he commissioned Baron Georges Eugène Haussmann to supervise such a project. Haussmann's Paris, as it gradually evolved, was the only lasting accomplishment of the emperor.

The demolition involved was ruthless, the reconstruction formidable. Eighty-five miles of new streets were added to the city scene, including great boulevards with wide carriageways and broad pavements lined with shade trees and with houses of prescribed height and facade —the *grands boulevards* that still so attractively dominate the plan of Paris. Many of the avenues were slashed through districts where the

A scene on the Champs-Élysées, by Constantin Guys

most restless workmen lived and made wide enough for cavalry troops to maneuver in, with military barracks at key points to discourage any further insurrections in such quarters.

But far beyond any strategic considerations, this gigantic transformation of the city was at once a magnificent imperial gesture and an urban renewal program of calculated economic consequence. Masons were brought in from the provinces and quickly put to work to supplement the local laboring forces; unskilled workmen became contractors by dint of sheer hard work. The emperor gave the bois de Boulogne to Paris, and Haussmann redesigned that dull royal forest as a handsomely landscaped park. Thus, also, Haussmann provided the city with the bois de Vincennes, the parc Monceau, and the parc des Buttes-Chaumont, those spacious and verdant oases where ever since children have played and adults have strolled or rested amid a profusion of flowering plants and tall trees.

Napoleon also called for a rejuvenation of the central marketing facilities of the city. "I want huge umbrellas, nothing more," he instructed Haussmann, and up went the cast-iron and glass structures, Les Halles, which served the city in picturesque fashion until very recent years. (The buildings still stand, but probably not for much longer.) One of Haussmann's most sensational achievements was underground. Before him, the sewers of Paris had been infamous; Victor Hugo's description of them in *Les Misérables* is unforgettable. Haussmann completely rebuilt the system, adding 500 miles of new water mains and 260 miles of new sewers; 32,000 gas lamps were installed to brighten the mighty scene.

The list of accomplishments seems almost endless. A finishing touch was to be the Opéra, designed by Charles Garnier, a resplendent structure decorated within and without in a giddy combination of styles. It is said that when the architect presented his plans to Napoleon, the empress asked, "And what is this style? It isn't Greek, it isn't Louis XIV, it isn't Louis XV." And Garnier replied, "It is Napoleon III, your Majesty. Are you complaining of that?" The remarkable structure was to have been the perfect setting for the splendor and luxury of Second Empire society, but it was not completed until after Louis Napoleon, Eugénie, and their court had left the scene.

Early in his reign as emperor, Louis had proclaimed *L'Empire c'est la paix,* "The empire stands for peace." In this he was not the best of prophets. During the Second Empire France waged four major wars and engaged in several minor military expeditions. Almost immediately after his pronouncement, France was involved with Turkey in the Crimean War against Russia, a dispute concerning the custody of holy places in Palestine. England joined France in what proved to be a blundering, highly unpopular conflict that ended with peace negotiations in Paris in 1856, after the allies had successfully raised the siege of Sebastopol. France gained nothing from that venture except some measure of military prestige, heavily paid for in lives and money. (One benefit was the Pont de l'Alma, opened by Louis Napoleon on April 2, 1856, in memory of the little river Alma, the crossing of which had freed the road to Sebastopol.)

Three years later, in 1859, after reaching a secret agreement with the Italian nationalist leader Cavour, the emperor himself led a French army into Italy to liberate that country from the Austrian forces that were threatening Piedmont and, in return for this help, to bring Savoy and Nice back within the "natural frontiers" of France. (That intervention also promised the opportunity of humbling the house of Hapsburg, a traditional French objective dating back to Richelieu.) However, the move led to difficulties from which Louis Napoleon was, in the end, unable to extricate himself. His troops won two quick, if costly, victories at Magenta and Solferino. Then a fresh surge of nationalism set off revolutions in the smaller Italian states. The revolt in the papal province of Romagna caused Eugénie, an ardent Roman Catholic, and the French clerical party, whose influence was strong in the nation, to protest against the consequences of French policy.

Prussia, with growing ambitions of its own, took sides against Italy and massed its forces along the Rhine. The emperor suddenly signed a truce with Austria, which alienated his Italian allies, and he advised the pope to yield to Italian nationalists, which further alienated the French clergy. He won nothing from his military venture but Savoy and Nice; he lost an important source of support at home—a loss that grew larger and more serious when a free trade treaty he secretly negotiated with Great Britain aroused the arrant opposition of the industrial bourgeoisie of France.

Alarmed by attacks from both clericals and capitalists, the emperor turned to the left for the support he had lost from the right. He edged toward a more liberal regime by removing the gag which had kept the country in silence and by reviving parliamentary life in the government. But his empire was in a decline that quickened with the failure of his foreign policies in the 1860s. For the most part, it is true, French colonial enterprise flourished—in Algeria, Senegal, Cochin China, Cambodia, and the Levant. In 1860, to demonstrate the superiority of European civilization, France joined England in a punitive force that looted Peking and burned the Summer Palace. And between 1859 and 1869 Ferdinand de Lesseps constructed the Suez Canal, a sensational accomplishment added to the prestige of France.

But, in 1862 France joined England and Spain in an ill-advised expedition to collect debts from a reformist government in Mexico that had repudiated loans incurred by its predecessors. The invasion was at best a sordid business involving venal private interests as well as imperialistic schemes. When England and Spain became aware of France's intent to establish a Catholic Latin empire in America they withdrew their forces. The remaining French troops were thereupon defeated in battle with the Mexicans. To avenge French honor and restore imperial dignity fresh reinforcements were then sent overseas and Mexico City was captured. (The United States, occupied with its own Civil War, failed to invoke the Monroe Doctrine.) Maximilian, a prince of Austria, was proposed as an enlightened despot to rule Mexico, and with the help of the French troops he was put on the throne with his wife Carlota at his side. However, with the end of the Civil War the United States insisted that the French withdraw. Unprotected by his French supporters Maximilian was shot by the Mexicans, Carlota went mad, and Napoleon's prestige suffered another damaging blow. What had been intended as the "greatest idea" of the emperor's reign led to his utter humiliation.

Between 1863 and 1867 Louis Napoleon had succeeded in alienating most of the important states in Europe. As one critic of the emperor exclaimed, "There are no blunders left for us to make." While nearly forty thousand first-line French troops were tied up across the Atlantic, the balance of power in Europe was changing. Across the French border Otto von Bismarck was scheming with cynical genius to build Prussia into the leading power among the German states—and of the

Sidewalk vendor offering rats for sale during the siege of Paris

Continent. In 1866 in a lightning campaign of a few weeks the Prussians defeated Austria. At a meeting with Bismarck in Biarritz, Napoleon had informally agreed to remain neutral in that conflict, expecting a lengthy war which he would finally mediate in return for territorial favors. Now he was facing a triumphant Prussia, practically supreme in the confederation of German states and heady with its power. Bismarck rebuffed all French claims for additional territory and Napoleon had added one more humiliation to his growing list.

Over the next four years both nations anticipated a conflict that seemed inevitable, a required step in the establishment of some realistic balance of power on the Continent. In 1870 Bismarck attempted to put a Hohenzollern prince, a relative of Wilhelm I, king of Prussia, on the throne of Spain. France was outraged at the prospect of being caught in a vise, with German rulers on her two opposite borders, and protested. To almost everyone's surprise, the Hohenzollern candidacy was consequently withdrawn. Wilhelm had no wish to precipitate war, and for the moment peace with honor seemed assured. Then France overplayed her hand by demanding that at no time in the future should the Prussian king reverse his decision. In a firm but courteous reply, Wilhelm refused to make any such commitment. However, his message was released to the press by Bismarck in an edited version that made it seem peremptory and arrogant, and that further wounded French pride. On July 19, 1870, France declared war on Prussia.

In an outburst of martial spirit French youths sang the *Marseillaise* in the streets of Paris; crowds shouted "On to Berlin!" Actually, France was not prepared for war. But Prussia was, and Bismarck's generals had agreed that it was in the German interest to precipitate the conflict at this time. As Bismarck had hoped, the other German states rallied to his leadership. With somewhat more reason for confidence than their French counterparts, crowds in the streets of Berlin shouted "On to Paris!"

Actually, the war was decided before the first shot was fired. Although he suffered from "a stone as big as a pigeon's egg" in his bladder, Napoleon took command of the French army. In his agony he could hardly sit his horse. His general staff and his military organization could not compare with the enemy's, and behind him at home he had only the hapless Eugénie as regent and an unpopular government.

German soldiers on the place de la Concorde, in Paris, May, 1871

Within weeks the emperor found himself surrounded at Sedan in the northeast of France and there, on September 2, he surrendered with almost 100,000 men. The war was not yet over, but with that defeat the Second Empire ended. Napoleon found his way to final exile in England and thence Eugénie, helped in her flight by an American dentist who practiced in Paris, followed him with their son.

A provisional government of National Defense was established in Paris and the National Guard was increased to more than a third of a million men. But the Germans quickly put a ring of 150,000 troops and 700 cannon around the city, virtually isolating it from the rest of the country. Balloons were used to carry individuals and messages out of the capital, but because of the prevailing westerly winds they could not return. Paris became a fortified camp. Without access to food or fuel

in the cold of winter the city held out for more than four months. Trees along the Champs-Élysées were cut down for firewood. Even so, as the Seine iced over, soldiers froze at their posts. Ragged citizens furtively grubbed for roots and green things in no man's land. As horses were slaughtered for their meat, even the Rothschilds had to go on foot to their destinations. The best restaurants served the meat of elephants and kangaroos from the city's zoo—even the meat of cats and rats from the city streets. Among the poorer classes cold and famine took a fearful toll. Then, for several hours each night for twenty-three nights, German batteries poured shells into the city from surrounding heights.

On January 28, 1871, Paris capitulated. Most of France was ready for peace. Ten days earlier in the Hall of Mirrors at Versailles, thanks to Bismarck's persistent efforts, the assembled German princes in full military regalia had proclaimed Wilhelm of Prussia the German emperor. He was now the most powerful ruler in Europe. By the terms of the peace treaty that was signed, France was obliged to cede most of Alsace and Lorraine to the new empire.

Shortly after the surrender of Paris a National Assembly assumed control of the French government and soon established its offices at Versailles—not at Paris. Out of its transactions eventually emerged the Third Republic. However, the people of Paris first had to suffer another siege, this time by their countrymen, and it was the bloodiest of all. On March 1, 1871, according to the terms of the treaty of peace, German troops marched triumphantly down the Champs-Élysées. It was a symbolic parade, but it enraged the Parisians, whose nerves were raw from their recent bitter trials. Paris wanted none of the Germans, none of the treaty, and none of the National Assembly (although that body had been elected by the nation at large). The city set up its own government, the Commune of 1871, aiming to decentralize France by enlarging the powers of municipalities. Then war broke out between Paris and Versailles.

The next few weeks were among the saddest in the long history of the capital. Troops controlled by the government at Versailles marched against the barricades that had once again been thrown up in the city's streets. Under the eyes of the victorious German forces, encamped on the heights overlooking the capitol, Frenchmen slaughtered Frenchmen in a frightful bath of blood. More people were killed

in one week than during the six years of the Revolution eighty years
before; no defeat in the war just ended had cost France so many lives.
The city itself suffered irreparable damages. The great column in the
place Vendôme was knocked down; the Tuileries palace, the venerable
and magnificent Hôtel de Ville, and other public and private buildings
were put to the torch in a last act of defiance by the desperate Communards. Resistance was finally crushed in the high grounds of the Père
Lachaise cemetery in an apocalyptic twilight. As the smoke from fires
in the city hung like a pall over the capital, the living fought a final
desperate battle among the tombs of the dead. When the carnage was
finally over France was left with a legacy of hatred between the right
and the left that has ever since poisoned French politics.

CHAPTER IX

A THIRD
REPUBLIC

*T*he Third Republic of France was born of the German invasion of 1870 and died with the German invasion of 1940. Between those dates it survived the German invasion of 1914. It proved to have been France's most durable regime since the demise of the old monarchy in 1792. However, during all its years the government was plagued by rivalry, at times intense and bitter, between two main opposing blocs: one that looked for firm authority, preferably in the form of a monarchy allied with the Church, the other that wanted a liberal republic and a complete separation of church and state. These were not political parties like the Republicans and Democrats in America, but loose agglomerations of factions polarized largely by the focal question of state-church relationships. In the uprisings of 1848 and 1871 their essential differences had been written out in the blood of opposing interests, leaving wounds that never completely healed.

France did not rush forward to embrace the Third Republic; she rather backed toward it. Following the so-called "bloody week" of May, 1871, the National Assembly gathered to settle the question of a new regime for France before its members dispersed. Almost two

Portrait of Gertrude Stein by Pablo Picasso, 1906

thirds of the members were monarchists, but this sizeable majority was sharply divided between adherents of the count of Chambord, the "legitimate" Bourbon contender, and those of the count of Paris, the Orleanist grandson of Louis Philippe. In the stalemate that resulted Adolphe Thiers was named "president of the Republic." Thiers had served as premier under Louis Philippe, he was an Orleanist at heart, he had directed the suppression of the Communards, and he was considered "safe" by the monarchists until they could resolve their differences and restore a king to the throne of France.

Thiers had more to offer than those qualifications of record. By shrewd and decisive measures he quickly paid off the huge indemnity which the Germans had imposed at the conclusion of the Franco-Prussian War, and thus relieved the country of the humiliating presence of the German occupation forces. The last German soldier moved out of France on September 16, 1873. Once again France had made a remarkable economic recovery in the wake of a disastrous war, a demonstration of basic resourcefulness that impressed Europe at large and alarmed the Germans in particular. Within a relatively few years after the Franco-Prussian War the nation could enter deliberation on equal terms with Germany. As early as 1872 the National Assembly passed a law embodying the principle of universal military service. Three years later a staff college, the École Supérieure de Guerre, was established— a French General Staff based on the Prussian model. Then a high command was organized to regulate military training during peace and to plan mobilization for war. It was enough to make Bismarck fearful, and he considered a preventive war before such preparations seriously threatened German security. But there was no real cause for such action before he was dismissed by Wilhelm II in 1890.

Once Thiers had accomplished his vital task he was forced to resign by the Assembly in favor of Marshal MacMahon, a veteran of past French wars and a staunch monarchist who, it was hoped, would help more effectively to pave the way to the restoration of the monarchy.

However, the stalemate among the would-be kingmakers continued and, to buy time, they extended the presidential powers of MacMahon to a period of seven years. But shortly, by 1875, it became apparent that the monarchists could not agree on their candidate. What was more, their position was threatened by a rising tide of radical republican sentiment from the left and a resurgent Bonapartism from the right. Rather than run the risk of losing control to either faction, the Assembly, in effect by a vote of 353 to 352, formally established the Third Republic and provided it with still another constitution. The very word *republic* was distasteful to many who voted in favor of establishing the new government. However, the constitution, as it was called, was actually a number of constitutional laws so framed as to leave open the possibility of an easy transition from republic to monarchy when circumstances favored such a change. Those circumstances never developed and, such as it was, the constitution of 1875 became the longest-lived of all the constitutions that the nation had contrived since the meeting of the Estates General in 1789. (It was the fourteenth since the Revolution of that year.)

The new government consisted of a chamber of deputies elected by universal, direct, male suffrage; a senate, or upper house, elected by indirect suffrage; and a president elected by both those bodies in joint session. A cabinet of ministers appointed by the president was responsible to the legislature for directing the general policy of the state. Without political parties organized about concerted programs, the cabinet usually represented precarious coalitions of assorted interests. If the cabinet and the legislature disagreed, as they repeatedly did over the years, it was the ministry that went out. Up until 1914 the average life of a French cabinet was one year. Meanwhile, under such circumstances, the president remained virtually a figurehead.

These arrangements satisfied no one completely; both left and right hoped to revise the various documents that made up the constitution the better to serve their separate interests. General elections held in 1876 returned a surprisingly large number of republicans to office, especially in the chamber—a swing to the left that disconcerted the conservatives. In 1877 the constitution was put to a crucial test that affected the whole life of the Third Republic when, using his presidential prerogatives, MacMahon dissolved the chamber. The ultimate point at issue was whether France was to have a presidential system of government, with a strong and independent chief executive, or a parliamentary system in which the elective legislature would assume the greater authority; the immediate question was whether the conservative, clerical faction would carry through a program aimed at restoring

the pope's temporal power—a program that could involve France in serious international difficulties.

In the ensuing elections the republicans came back with a clear majority; the principle of ministerial responsibility triumphed over that of the personal power of the president; and, shortly afterward, a series of anticlerical decrees were passed. (The Jesuits were ordered to disband and disperse and all other religious teaching associations were abolished.) Following that abortive *coup d'état* by MacMahon and his supporters, no French president ever again dared to dissolve the chamber of deputies during the rest of the history of the Third Republic. (The president in subsequent years has been described as "an elderly gentleman, whose function it was to wear evening dress in day-time.") For the next forty years the republicans dominated French politics. Significantly, the seat of government was moved from Versailles back to Paris; the *Marseillaise* was made the national anthem; and the fourteenth of July was decreed a national holiday. The inscription "Liberté, Égalité, Fraternité" reappeared on all public buildings.

"The Proclamation of the Third Republic," September 4, 1870

In the midst of the turbulent political scene the life of the nation progressed at other levels with wholesome vigor, even with brilliance. On February 5, 1875, while contesting forces were bitterly thrashing out the details of the new constitution, Marshal MacMahon officially opened the Opéra, planned so long before by Napoleon III as one of the great cultural monuments to his reign. By this time the emperor had died in exile, but his intentions were magnificently realized by the architect Garnier. The Opéra was the largest theater in the world, and no pains had been spared to make it the most resplendent. Variously colored marbles from all the quarries of France were used for its walls, floors, and other architectural elements. Seventy-three sculptors and thirteen painters had been commissioned to ornament the structure under Garnier's direction. (The famous dancing group on the facade was executed by the architect's friend Jean Baptiste Carpeaux.) A glittering chandelier weighing six tons hung in the theater; the foyer and great staircases became a stage for France's most brilliant society.

In 1878, seven years after the crushing defeat by Germany and the

Caricature of Victor Hugo amid scenes suggesting his famous works

wholesale slaughter of the Communard riots, France celebrated its complete recovery from the disasters of war and strife with a Universal Exhibition held in Paris. It was the first public rejoicing since those dire events. On the bluffs of Chaillot overlooking the Seine (a site called Trocadéro from the name of a fort in the Bay of Cádiz taken by French troops in 1823) a huge pavilion in a vaguely Hispano-Moorish style was raised, a monumental fantasy that remained standing, regarded with affectionate indulgence by most old Parisians, until it was replaced in 1937 by the present Palais de Chaillot.

Two years before this celebration, work had started on the basilica of Sacré Coeur on the heights of Montmartre, where Saint Denis had been martyred so many centuries before, where Ignatius Loyola and his first group of followers had taken vows in 1534 (the members of the Society of Jesus), and where the blood of the Communards had been shed so recently. In the days immediately following the troubles of 1870 and 1871, a popular religious movement appealed for the erection of such a shrine, to be built by national subscriptions, as a symbol of contrition for the sins of the past and of hope for the future. In 1873, by a large majority, the National Assembly declared that this was a matter of public utility, no doubt linking the sorrows of France with those of the Church, whose head was then a prisoner of the Vatican and whose liberation was the concern of all devout Catholics in the Assembly as elsewhere. The great white structure which, along with the Eiffel Tower, dominates the skyline of Paris, was finally dedicated in 1919, one year after another and far more frightful bloodletting that had again left France devastated.

Meanwhile, in 1874, France underwent another, bloodless revolution. In that year a group of artists, despairing of ever winning recognition at the official salons of the French Academy—a matter of professional life or death for many of them—held their first independent exhibition. Eleven years earlier Napoleon III, partly as a political move in response to certain complaints, had authorized a second salon for the display of pictures rejected by the jury. But this *Salon des Réfusés,* as it was called, was neither a critical nor a popular success, although it did expose to public view paintings that would otherwise have long remained unknown. Three paintings by Manet were hung there, for example, including his celebrated "Déjeuner sur l'herbe," which the emperor called immodest and which was eagerly acquired by the Louvre some years later. (The other two Manet paintings now hang in the Metropolitan Museum of Art.)

Manet did not join the independents of 1874 (he coveted salon recognition), but among those who did were other talents that would later be considered among the greatest of the century—Boudin, Cézanne, Degas, Monet, Morisot, Pissarro, Renoir, and Sisley. They were a mixed group without a descriptive name. However, almost at once the public derisively dubbed them Impressionists, a name considered as funny as Monet's painting, "Impression—Sunrise," that had suggested it. Soon the artists themselves accepted that designation, calling their group *Peintres Impressionistes.* Their main point was to win the right to paint what and how they pleased without deference to the Academy's inbred and fusty standards of value, and to attract the attention of dealers and collectors by the merits of their individual work. In this they succeeded. The stranglehold of the Academy was finally broken.

Over the decade and a half following the overthrow of the Second Empire public regard for Victor Hugo grew almost to the point of idolatry. Because of his opposition to Napoleon, Hugo had been exiled from France; in 1870 he returned to Paris in triumph. He was elected to the National Assembly and the senate, and he continued to write novels that added to his fame. On February 26, 1881, to pay homage to him on his eightieth birthday, more than a half million Parisians coursed past his house on the avenue d'Eylau, a street that was then renamed avenue Victor Hugo. When the great man died four years later, his body lay in state under the Arc de Triomphe, watched over by twelve young poets. There, wrote Romain Rolland, "the god slept like a conqueror, on the field of glory snatched from his great rival Napoleon," before the remains, accompanied by two million Frenchmen, were borne to the Pantheon for interment. Before the end of the obsequies public excitement had approached delirium. A later generation of critics would move in to whittle away at the reputation of the great poet and novelist.

A few months after Hugo's death Louis Pasteur and his assistants cured a small boy of rabies with the vaccine they had developed. People who had been bitten by mad dogs came from everywhere to Paris to be saved. Nineteen men who had been attacked by a mad wolf came from

The Eiffel Tower, the world's tallest structure when erected in 1889

the farther reaches of Russia. The consistent success of the vaccine in treating the dreaded disease led to an international subscription for the establishment in 1888 of the Pasteur Institute.

But not even Pasteur's genius could halt the spread of the grape phylloxera, a grievous pest that was devastating French vineyards. That insect had first appeared in the department of Gard, in Languedoc, in 1860, apparently introduced either on table grapes or in rootstocks imported from America, where phylloxera is native. By 1868 the vines of Bordeaux had been attacked; by 1870, the year of the war with Prussia, the insect invasion had spread to Beaujolais and the Rhone valley. (It has been said that damage from phylloxera cost France more than twice the amount Bismarck demanded as indemnity.) By 1884 virtually the entire wine industry of the country faced utter ruin. The plague was halted only when three or four million acres of vineyards were completely uprooted and replanted with imported American stocks which had grown resistant to phylloxera, and French vines then grafted on them. Whether pre-phylloxera French wines are better than those produced from grafted vines remains a point of refined debate among experts. However, a vital industry had been saved, and, in any case, French wines remain incomparable.

During this period France occupied a singular position as a republic in an otherwise monarchical Europe. But the monarchist tradition was not yet dead in France. It had persisted while the Republic approached the age at which all previous regimes since 1789 had been overthrown. To the public at large the government began to seem uninspired, its

"They've sworn not to discuss the Dreyfus affair." "They've discussed it."

representatives fat with the perquisites of office. One cartoon depicted
the Republic as a tired, faded, female figure wearing a liberty cap, regarded by an elderly café philosopher who wistfully observes: "How beautiful she was under the Empire!" In 1883 Prince Napoleon, son of the first emperor's brother Jerome and head of the Bonaparte family, published posters demanding a plebiscite, which he overconfidently thought might restore his political future. But the posters were censored and he was thereupon exiled along with all members of families that had reigned in France. Even so, in the elections of 1885 almost 50 per cent of the votes went to monarchists; Frenchmen on both the left and the right were disenchanted by the bumbling mediocrity of parliamentary rule. Specific causes of discontent were put forward—an agricultural depression (especially in the wine-exporting regions), a scandal involving the president's son-in-law, and a lingering, unpopular war in Indochina.

Against this background appeared General Georges Boulanger, a handsome and soldierly figure who, astride his black charger Tunis (Boulanger was a veteran of the Tunis campaign), seemed to many like a man of destiny. The mass of people responded to that image; broadsides and ballads made his name and features familiar everywhere. Monarchists and Bonapartists also thought they saw in him the instrument they needed for their cause. The passionately royalist—and very rich—duchess of Uzès backed him financially; he paid a secret visit to the exiled Prince Napoleon; he had some support from the Church and the army.

An apprehensive republican government removed Boulanger first from his position as minister of war, then from his military command, thus making him a sort of martyr. Now free to run for political office, he waged a fiery campaign and won repeated victories in regional polls. When he was triumphantly elected as a member for the metropolitan department of the Seine by a large majority in Paris in January, 1889, his rise to power seemed certain. His partisans shouted "To the Élysée." A royalist *coup d'état* seemed in the making. But at that critical moment Boulanger declined to take the initiative. It was a watershed in the history of French politics. The republicans rallied, issued a warrant for his arrest charging him with conspiracy, and the ex-hero fled the country. On September 30, 1891, in a melodramatic anticlimax to his career, Boulanger took his life at the tomb of his mistress in Brussels. By his precipitate flight, it could be said, he had saved the Republic which had done so little to save itself.

A brief period of calm followed this crisis. In the general elections of 1889 the republicans regained much of the ground they had lost in 1885. Also, in 1889, France held another universal exhibition to celebrate the centenary of the Revolution, and the Eiffel Tower, the world's tallest and most daring structure, rose on the Left Bank of the Seine opposite the Trocadéro, to vie with the towers of Notre Dame as a commanding feature of the Paris skyline—a very symbol of the city.

The year 1891 was one of the few in the history of the Third Republic without a change of ministry. Then in quick succession two new political storms threatened to topple the Republic. In 1892 survivors of the Boulangist movement and other conservative elements found an opening to attack the government through the failure of the Panama Canal Company (Compagnie du Canal Interocéanique), in which fiasco a number of highly placed republican politicians were implicated. The company, formed to cut a canal through the Isthmus of Panama, was headed by Ferdinand de Lesseps, the respected promoter of the Suez Canal. The project ran into extraordinary and unprecedented difficulties and, having exhausted its resources, the company floated a bond issue that required the authorization of parlement— which it got by devious means. Even so, it went bankrupt without accomplishing its goal, and many small investors lost their savings. In the resulting investigation scores of government officials and the editors of national papers, as well as the entrepreneurs, were charged with complicity in having received payments for passing the legislation required for the bond issue and for having deceived the public. The legal outcome was an anticlimax. Only a handful of those judged were found guilty. Challenged and embarrassed as it was, the republican government survived the scandal. By the time the matter was settled, ironically, the construction difficulties of the canal were being resolved. After fomenting a revolution in Panama the remaining promoters sold their interest to the United States.

Less than a year after the Panama Canal incident, another scandal rocked the Republic on its foundations. On October 15, 1894, Captain Alfred Dreyfus, a probationer in the intelligence section of the general

staff of the French army, was charged with treason for having delivered
military secrets to the Germans. Dreyfus protested his innocence, but
in secret session a court-martial sentenced him to life imprisonment on
Devil's Island off the coast of French Guiana. Dreyfus was the son of a
Jewish manufacturer of Alsace, the first Jew ever to have been a member of the general staff. The army was traditionally royalist, Catholic,
and to a large degree anti-Semitic. This fact played a part not only in
Dreyfus' conviction but in the subsequent development of the case.

In 1896 an army officer produced evidence indicating that Dreyfus
had been the victim of a forgery and was in fact completely innocent
of the charge brought against him. But that information was suppressed by the authorities; neither the government nor the army wished
to be exposed to embarrassment. However, the next year Dreyfus'
brother independently discovered the same evidence and then the case
burst into the open. Almost immediately French society was divided
into two apparently irreconcilable factions, the Dreyfusards and the
anti-Dreyfusards. Opinions tended to polarize about basic differences
in outlook that did not necessarily have anything to do with the merits
of the Dreyfus case. Royalist, militant, and some other elements found
it possible to believe that Dreyfus was guilty; republican, socialist,
and anticlerical elements felt they had enough proof that he was innocent. The controversy carried beyond the limits of political and religious considerations; it disrupted French life even at the family level.
One contemporary cartoon showed a decorous family gathering, over
the caption, "They've sworn not to discuss the Dreyfus affair"; the adjoining picture showed the same group assaulting one another without
mercy over the caption, "They've discussed it."

Men in high places seem to have put their piety and patriotism above
truth and justice and perjured themselves. The popular author Émile
Zola, on the other hand, was sentenced to jail for issuing a protest
against Dreyfus' incrimination, and fled to England. The nation
seemed on the verge of civil war in disagreement over this one question; street clashes were frequent. Then, in 1899, Dreyfus was granted
a pardon by the president of the Republic. But it was not until 1906
that he was finally and completely exonerated.

With all its sordid and divisive aspects the Dreyfus affair occupied
the middle years of a period that was otherwise fondly remembered as

OVERLEAF: *"Le Déjeuner sur l'herbe," painted by Edouard Manet in 1863*

la belle époque—"the good old days" around the turn of the century. In spite of bitter internal dissensions France enjoyed peace and prosperity during those years. Haussmann had left Paris looking more beautiful than ever. The city was the world's playground, the haunt of such figures as the Prince of Wales and the king of the Netherlands and of many other titled, wealthy foreigners. Eugénie no longer reigned over the social scene, but France had a new queen in Sarah Bernhardt. In 1875 the "divine Sarah" became a member of the Comédie Française and she took Paris for her personal stage. For sixty-one tumultuous years, in which she played two hundred roles, she put on a continuous, prodigious performance, on and off stage, that captured the attention of the whole world.

During those years of the Third Republic Paris was also the cultural capital of the world. "Inevitable Paris beckoned," wrote Henry Adams of his life just after the turn of the century, "and resistance became more and more futile as the store of years grew less; for the world contains no other spot than Paris where education can be pursued from every side. Even more vigorously than in the twelfth century, Paris taught in the twentieth, with no other school approaching it for variety of direction and energy of mind. . . . Scores of artists—sculptors and painters, poets and dramatists, workers in gems and metals, designers in stuffs and furniture—hundreds of chemists, physicists, even philosophers, philologists, physicians, and historians—were at work, a thousand times as actively as ever before, and the mass and originality of their products would have swamped any previous age, as it nearly swamped its own."

The Impressionists had triumphed over their earlier difficulties and were winning increasing public acceptance; they had become the "founders" of modern art, had paved the way for a new generation of talents. Late in the century the crippled little aristocrat Henri de Toulouse-Lautrec immortalized in paintings, prints, and posters, the singers and dancers of the day—Yvette Guilbert, Jane Avril, and the others, and portrayed the life of bars and brothels in *fin de siècle* Paris. Cézanne, the greatest innovator in Western painting since Giotto six centuries earlier, won his first public recognition (at the age of sixty-one) at the centennial exhibition of 1900—the year Pablo Picasso came for the first time from Spain to Paris, where he was to succeed

A photograph of Henri Toulouse-Lautrec and a model among his paintings

Cézanne as a great seminal influence in art for the next two generations. Modigliani came from Italy in 1906, Chagall from Russia in 1910. The whole world contributed to the School of Paris.

The Third Republic also had its own school of music, although Berlin, even after the death of the "godlike" Wagner, remained the musical capital of Europe. In 1892 Claude Debussy composed *The Afternoon of a Faun* and ten years later *Pelléas and Mélisande*. From 1872 until his death in 1890 César Franck, professor of organ at the Paris Conservatory, completed his mature works. Saint-Saëns wrote his great Third Symphony in 1886. Diaghilev brought a company of Russian dancers to Paris in 1909, and four years later Igor Stravinsky's ballet *The Rites of Spring* had its premiere in Paris, with the great Nijinsky on stage.

In the sciences the work of Pasteur, Berthelot, Henri Poincaré, the Curies, and others had won France an international reputation equaling that which it held in the arts. Zola, Taine, Anatole France, Guy de Maupassant, André Gide, and Marcel Proust, to mention but a few, remain great names in the literary history of the Third Republic. Proust was born with the Third Republic in 1871. Only the first volume of his great work, *À la recherche du temps perdu,* was published before the First World War, in 1913. When he completed that series shortly after the war, it became apparent that he had with rare genius recorded the end of an era.

In the first decade of the twentieth century France had every reason to be proud of its achievements and of the prestige it had won among the nations of the world. That a golden era was ending was not then apparent. The Republic seemed to be approaching an unprecedented stability. A wave of anarchism and other problems caused by a sharp rise in trade unionism, with its attendant disruptive strikes, plagued the government from the left. (In 1902 the Confederation of Labor— the Confédération Générale du Travail, or "C.G.T.," as it continues to be popularly known under its present-day Communist leadership—became the official spokesman for French labor, advocating violence, sabotage, and the "general strike," as the necessary weapons of its membership.) From the right the government was assailed by the exasperated conservative forces that had staked so much on finally establishing the guilt of Dreyfus. L'Action Française was organized in 1899,

advocating a militant policy called "integral nationalism," extolling
France above all other nations. The members of that faction called for
a more firm authority than they felt could be exercised by parliamentary
democracy, and in their propaganda the menace of modern right-wing
totalitarian ideology was discernible.

In spite of those tensions the Republic endured. Its essential stability
depended on an efficient administrative corps that continued to perform its functions through all changes in the legislative body. The
conclusion of the Dreyfus affair had strengthened the antimilitaristic
and anticlerical sentiment among the French people, as reflected in
their choice of legislators. In 1906 the electorate solemnly ratified a
law finally separating church and state, ending that long "marriage of
inconvenience" which Napoleon had instituted with the Concordat of
1801—and which he himself had come to consider one of his worst
mistakes. Freed from the trammels of government regulation, the
Church in France enjoyed a revival of thought and spirit that was
clearly manifested in the Catholic literature and architecture of the
next decades.

It was during the Third Republic, in the last quarter of the nineteenth century, that France developed colonial holdings second in extent and importance only to those of Great Britain. French colonial
enterprise dates back to the eleventh and twelfth centuries when, it
could be said, England and the Holy Lands were dependencies of
France. Many centuries later vast areas in North America had been
acquired, and then lost. By the end of the reign of Napoleon Bonaparte
France retained but a small fraction of her whilom far-flung colonial
holdings. However, with the Second Empire the conquest of Algeria,
begun under Louis Philippe, was completed, and a firm foothold was
gained in Indochina. Then, within a decade or so after the Franco-
Prussian War, the pace of overseas expansion quickened.

In 1881, following a Machiavellian suggestion by Bismarck, the
former Barbary state of Tunis was brought under French protection.
(This move forestalled an Italian advance into that area, and in wrath
over the French action, Italy almost immediately entered a Triple Alliance with Germany and Austria-Hungary to prevent French aggression
in Central Europe.) Shortly after that development a police action
undertaken in Indochina turned into a full-blown war which, as it

dragged on with a mounting toll of deaths in that unhealthy region halfway round the globe, dismayed the French public—and obviously gratified Bismarck. However, in 1887 Cochin China, Annam, Cambodia, and Tonkin were all successfully brought together under colonial administration as French Indochina, to remain for two generations the greatest of French colonies. (Laos was added to that union in 1893.)

In the meantime, another series of colonial wars was extending French rule in Africa to Timbuktu, to the Congo basin, and northward toward the Nile. Vast areas, including French Guiana, Senegal, the Ivory Coast, French Equatorial Africa, and Mauritania were taken over. With Algeria, Tunisia, and Morocco to the north, and intervening territories, these colonies covered almost a third of the enormous continent. Finally, the island of Madagascar, off the southeast coast of Africa, was added to these bulging dominions. The Republic had created an empire.

War with Germany remained a major threat to the accomplishments of the Third Republic. Colonial expansion in Asia and, especially, Africa had brought France into direct conflict with both Germany and Great Britain. In 1904 an agreement was reached whereby France, reluctantly, recognized Great Britain's rights in Egypt in exchange for French freedom of action in Morocco. Germany was not pleased, and in 1905 and again in 1912 crises arose over the Moroccan problem. France, Great Britain, and Russia allied themselves to confront a German-Austrian-Italian alliance, and war was in the making. Significant elements of the French population had never been reconciled to the loss of Alsace and Lorraine, considered to be France's "natural" territories in 1871. However, the prevailing sentiment of the nation was pacific up to the moment when the call to arms was sounded in August, 1914. When Germany declared war in that month French opinion crystallized and the differences that had strained the Republic over the preceding decades were forgotten in a surge of nationalism. President Raymond Poincaré's appeal for a *union sacrée* had been heeded.

If the people of France at large had not looked forward to the prospect of war with Germany, the French general staff had done so, as had its German counterpart. The military high commands of both nations were prepared to fight a sharp offensive war that by their separate calculations could, like the war of 1870, be won in a few months' time.

According to plan French troops quickly invaded the "lost provinces" of Alsace and Lorraine, where their blue coats and red trousers made bright targets for the German machine guns that were awaiting them. Initial losses were so grave that retreat was imperative. Meanwhile, the main, gray-clad German army, disregarding Belgium's neutrality, swept through that country with the intention of swinging eastward around Paris and driving the French army up into Germany. France would thus be crushed before her Russian allies had time to advance on Germany from the east.

That possibility was menacing enough for the French government to flee Paris for Bordeaux. Then, reinforced by troops rushed to the front from Paris in taxicabs, the French army turned on the invaders and at the first battle of the Marne staved off their advance. Paris was saved by what became known as the Miracle on the Marne. Following that halt to the German advance, contingents of both armies raced westward in a vain effort to outflank one another. Soon the front line of conflict stretched from the sea to the Alps and, contrary to every expectation, the opposing forces had dug in for what was to be four exhausting and frightful years of trench warfare. Although millions of men lost their lives over that period, only a scant few miles of shell-torn ground ever changed hands.

Buttressed by barbed wire and machine guns, defenses on both sides were practically impregnable. Every attacking force exposed itself to a murderous barrage that bled it white. The point was made with ghastly emphasis in two great battles of 1916. At Verdun, the Germans' unsuccessful assault on that fortress cost them almost a quarter of a million men, and the French somewhat more; but Verdun was not taken. That same year the British Expeditionary Forces launched an offensive on the Somme River in northwestern France, and lost 60 per cent of their officers and 40 per cent of their rank and file on the first day. When the battle was over more than a million men on both sides were dead or wounded, and the British had advanced no more than seven miles. Such carnage was unheard of, unthinkable. The drainage of manpower was particularly serious for the French. France had long been the most populous nation in Europe, but by 1914 the German Empire numbered half again as many people and, grim as the statistics were, could survive the greater toll.

In its measure the French home front also experienced the war at first hand. As early as August, 1914, German planes had appeared over Paris, and they were followed by raiding Zeppelins and still other planes dropping bombs and aerial torpedoes. Later, in March, 1918, Paris awakened to the sound and sight of large shells bursting in the streets, fired from the region of Laon, some seventy miles to the north, by a gigantic cannon called Big Bertha after Frau Bertha Krupp, proprietor of the works where the huge weapon was made. On Good Friday that year one shell hit the church of Saint-Gervais in the heart of the capital during the evening service, killing seventy-four worshipers and injuring many more. But by then, partly because fresh American troops were reaching the front, the tide of the war was turning. Eight months later Germany surrendered, and in June, 1919, forty-eight years after Bismarck had proclaimed the German Empire in the Hall of Mirrors at Versailles, Germany signed the treaty of peace, dictated by the Allies, in that same chamber.

France had survived an ordeal of unprecedented horror. The final victory of the Allies had been won under the supreme command of a French general. The French people had responded to the demands of

its republican government with services and sacrifices such as no absolute monarch could possibly have commanded and obtained. In spite
of its trials the government retained its form and authority. Alsace and
Lorraine had at last been retrieved from alien control. Names of illustrious heroes and patriots, like Foch and Clemenceau, had emerged
from the strife as new symbols of France's glory; the Marne and Verdun had become sites to be forever associated with French resistance
to oppression. And with the war's end France seemed to have regained
hegemony on the Continent.

However, the price of survival and victory had been formidable.
Almost a million and a half soldiers and a half million civilians were
dead, or soon would be, and three quarters of a million more were
permanently disabled. The war had been fought largely on French soil,
with the Germans occupying some of the most important agricultural
and industrial areas of the land—areas that had been looted and devastated. (Without substantial help from the fields and factories of Great
Britain and the Americas France could not have endured.) Priceless
cultural monuments had been destroyed. Enormous national debts had
been incurred. The bitter consequences of such experiences would be
felt for decades to come.

The major objective of French statesmanship following the war was
the containment of Germany who, even in defeat, remained stronger
than France herself. Twice in the past fifty years France had been attacked by Germany, and before that, from the beginning of her national
existence, she had been plagued by Germanic invasions. There is not
space here to detail the policies France pursued in a futile effort to gain
her ends. And it is hardly necessary to recall that French cynicism in
this regard, which was so much stronger than the divergent opinions
held by her allies at the peace table, was unhappily justified. Within
twenty years the hordes descended from the north once again, this time
in overwhelming force.

Internally, during the interval between the wars France attempted
to put its own battered house in order, but there was no solid agreement as to how that might best be done—a sorry truth clearly indicated
by the fact that in those twenty years there were forty-three different
ministries, with an average lifetime of 170 days for each. The Third
Republic continued but the *sacrée union* of the war years had dissolved;

A German corpse on the Somme battlefield, 1916

its institutions were seriously attacked from both the left and the right. On the left, the Socialist Party split into two factions, one of which joined the Communist International, looked to Moscow for direction, and called for a dictatorship of the proletariat; on the right, some reactionary Frenchmen saw in the example of Italian fascism hope that a totalitarian government might settle the ills of the nation.

Tensions generated by opposing political groups within the nation threatened to wreck the parliamentary system altogether. In 1934 a relatively minor scandal, the Stavisky Affair, which revealed corruption in government circles, caused a violent public demonstration. Mobs collected in the streets and the police fired upon them; it recalled the days of the Commune. Although the crowds had no apparent concerted purpose, the incident could have been construed as an attempted *coup d'état* by the right. This possibility was enough to weld all the parties of the left—Communists, Socialists, and Radicals—into what was called the Popular Front, in opposition to the forces of reaction. The combination won a handsome victory at the polls in 1936 and brought the Socialist leader Léon Blum to the premiership. A series of long-overdue reforms, including compulsory arbitration of labor disputes, the forty-hour work week, and vacations with pay, were put into effect. For a moment it seemed to the mass of Frenchmen that the Republic was young and dynamic again. Conservatives believed that a revolution had been averted. Actually the effect of the Popular Front was to polarize opinion to the left and to the right at the expense of the center, creating an uneasy balance of factional interest. France was reacting in a particular way to the force of external circumstances as well as internal developments. Less than ever before could France isolate herself from, no less direct, as she once did, the forces that were shaping and changing the world about her.

La belle époque had vanished forever in the gunsmoke of 1914. Yet even during the years of war Paris remained a magnet for those who sought excitement, entertainment, and stimulation. American troops returned home singing songs of "gay Paree," a city of such attractions as few of them had ever before known. Following the armistice, the city quickly resumed its role as world capital of elegance and pleasure, of art and learning—a gathering place for writers, artists, and intellectuals. The American author Gertrude Stein came to live in Paris, to conduct an influential salon there, and to become the friend and patroness of Matisse and Picasso, among others. Ernest Hemingway and F. Scott Fitzgerald found their way to her house and heard her criticisms. American students took courses at the ancient Sorbonne. The University recovered its medieval glory as "the second light of the world" and, as in the Middle Ages, many nations built residential halls in neighboring streets. (Others came to France to find employment or to find refuge from oppression in their own lands. Between the two wars France received more immigrants than the United States.)

Proust, Gide, Cocteau, Duhamel, and Giraudoux were among the shining lights in a constellation of literary talents. Ladies of French society sent their valets in advance to secure seats in courses given by the celebrated philosopher Henri Bergson at the Collège de France. The couturier Paul Poiret delighted ladies of all lands with his creations. Tourists from everywhere thronged to the Casino de Paris and the Moulin Rouge to see and hear Maurice Chevalier and Mistinguette, among other memorable performers. In preparation for the International Exhibition of 1937 the old Palais du Trocadéro was demolished to make room for the new Palais de Chaillot, a virtual city of museums as it now stands on its bluff overlooking the gardens of the Trocadéro, the Seine, and, across the river, the Eiffel Tower and the Champ de Mars. The realization of that grouping of buildings and vistas was the most original and grandiose accomplishment in architectural planning of the period.

Life was a pageant of inexhaustible variety as the twenties drifted into the thirties—and as the thirties drifted toward the catastrophe of the next great war. In the years immediately preceding the outbreak of that war, France seemed to be in the grip of forces, both domestic and foreign, paralyzing any action that might have averted disaster; she was locked in a tight pattern of world-wide problems, most of them not of her making or wanting; and she was not morally ready for war. The generation that ruled the country in 1939 had known victory and had learned how little it meant in itself, except as the avoidance of defeat. Now, in the words of D. W. Brogan, they were to learn the price of not avoiding it. When the Nazis sent their divisions around the end of the "impregnable" Maginot Line, the Third Republic, weakened by bitter internal feuds, had in effect finally come to its end.

CHAPTER X

PAST, PRESENT, AND FUTURE

he German army invaded the Low Countries on May 10, 1940, and marched triumphantly into Paris just five weeks later. Nothing like that "blitzkrieg" had been known in the history of warfare. France was stunned, bewildered. An armistice was signed with Germany on June 22 and with Italy two days later. (Like a jackal impatient to feed at a still twitching carcass, Italy had attacked France from the rear in the last days of the Nazi onslaught—as soon as it was certain that France was already beaten.) Hitler, with his earlier conquests of Poland and Finland, now controlled virtually all western Europe, and could dance with glee atop the Eiffel Tower, while Parisians wept below.

During the course of the very brief struggle, when her cause was already lost, France had recalled the aging hero of Verdun, Marshal Pétain, to bolster the nation's morale, and with the resignation of President Renaud, Pétain became the leader of the wartime government. "At such a time of disaster," writes Robert Aron, ". . . France, as her only resource, had but an old man, laden with glory and years, who still remembered having learned his catechism from a chaplain who

Icarus in a colored paper cutout composition by Henri Matisse, 1947

had been a veteran of the Grand Army." Pétain was eighty-four years old; it was he who decided that France must sue for peace and make the best of its bitter defeat. A much younger general, Charles de Gaulle, who had escaped to England, appealed to his countrymen to continue the resistance. "France has lost a battle," he said. "But France has not lost the war." However, he then commanded but a handful of supporters, and did not enjoy the full confidence of Churchill and Roosevelt.

Pétain remained the nominal head of the French government, with headquarters at Vichy, until France was liberated in 1944. He was recognized as such by the Allies, although most of his authority gradually passed to that archcollaborationist Pierre Laval, who expected, wanted, and hoped to profit from Germany's ultimate victory over the Allies. The American ambassador described Pétain as a "feeble, frightened, old man, surrounded by self-seeking conspirators."

During the last years of the war the French people were subjected to an almost insupportable burden of hunger, terror, and devastation. As the chance of an ultimate German victory diminished, Nazi determination to drain France of its resources and manpower grew more desperate. Increased German demands for food reduced many Frenchmen to a starvation diet. Units of the French army were sent to the Russian front to fight the Soviets. By the autumn of 1943 almost two thirds of a million French men and women had been conscripted to help with German war production. Many never returned.

Growing resistance within France incited the Nazis and some of their French supporters to a mounting campaign of gruesome retaliation. Countermeasures by the French resistance added to the terror and the bloodletting. After 1942, it is said, attacks on individuals by one side or the other amounted to one hundred a day. Mass killings by the Germans were not uncommon. On June 10, 1944, German agents rounded up some six hundred women and children, confined them in the little church of Oradour-sur-Glane, and put a torch to the building. As liberation approached Allied bombers and invading forces brought even more death and destruction to a land already ravaged.

When France was free again her plight seemed catastrophic. Almost two million houses had been damaged, one half million of them beyond repair. The railways were in a state of virtual ruin. Three thousand bridges were destroyed. Nine tenths of the former total number of vehicles were not roadworthy—and there was not enough gasoline for those that were. Airfields were deeply pitted and there were no French planes suitable to carry on necessary communications. Radio stations had been destroyed and telegraph and telephone lines cut. Factories had been stripped of their machinery. Vast areas of fertile ground had been sown with mines. Most French ports were in ruins; great cities such as Rouen were largely reduced to rubble; and almost all the lovely cathedral towns of Normandy were frightfully disfigured.

France had to rebuild both a devastated economy and a shattered political organization. Following the liberation the nation once again demonstrated its powers of recuperation, as it had in 1871 and 1919. This time, to be sure, substantial American aid was an important factor in the recovery. In any event, by 1951 industrial production had already regained its pre-war peak, and six years later it stood at double the 1938 level. The nation was headed for greater prosperity than ever before. With the peace a considerable part of the economy was quickly nationalized—some public utilities, the coal mines, Air France, and the Renault automobile works, among other key industries. (The railways, armaments, and to a degree the Bank of France had been taken over by the Popular Front government before the war. Today about half of all French investment is controlled by the state.)

In political matters France soon resumed its pre-war pattern. When the first general elections were held in October, 1945, the results were what might have been expected had there been no war. Between them, the Communists and the Socialists almost won a majority, as in the 1936 elections that had been dominated by the Popular Front. By a vote of twenty to one the French people repudiated the Third Republic. With a new constitution, under a new republic, it was widely hoped, France would have a fresh start and could forget the corruption, the misery, and the defeat of the recent past. That was an illusion very soon to be dispelled. By virtually unanimous agreement, De Gaulle, who had exercised emergency powers following the liberation, was elected provisional president until the new government could be formally instituted. But within a few months, disagreeing with the Constituent Assembly on the question of his executive power and dismayed by the strife among party politicians, he resigned the post "irrevocably."

Under other leadership the Fourth Republic was duly launched in November, 1946, and thereupon the familiar round of changing ministries was resumed with an even quicker turnover than before the war. Government instability became all but ludicrous. There were nine different ministries in the next five years; one lasted two days, another a month. In spite of all its weaknesses and hazards, the Third Republic had lasted for three quarters of a century; the Fourth Republic barely survived a dozen years.

It would be tedious to detail the makeshift coalitions of various factions—of Communists, Socialists, Catholics, democrats, Gaullists, and still others—that attempted unsuccessfully to provide France with a firm government during the brief life of the Fourth Republic. The new constitution was at best a feeble compromise of disparate interests. In France no single party has been strong enough to form a government on its own strength alone, as the Democrats and Republicans do in America. Generally speaking, each of the major political parties in America has drawn its support from all classes, sections, and interests within the country; neither could afford to differ too radically from the other without sacrificing some important element of public support. The French parliamentary government rather reflected the internal divisions within the country—regional differences and differences between town and country, between Catholics on the one hand and Protestants or secular interests on the other, or between the different classes of the populace. The continued instability of the successive governments discouraged Frenchmen from conceding that any one in that passing parade in the end represented rightful and final authority.

Whatever the nature of internal problems, post-war French policies were more than ever before shaped by pressures from abroad. Of all French political parties the Communist was the most highly disciplined, and at times the largest. To a nation dependent for the time on American aid, this was an embarrassment as the conflict between the Western powers and the Soviet Union congealed into the Cold War. In May, 1947, the Communists were eliminated from the coalition government that had been formed after the adoption of the new constitution. Despite the violent opposition of both Communists and left-wing Socialists, in 1949 France joined fourteen other nations—soon including West Germany—in signing the North Atlantic Treaty, a defensive al-

liance (NATO) to be financed and armed principally by the United States. It was an important commitment for France, for the agreement implied that a revived, substantially armed Germany would have to play a part in the defense of western Europe—enough to worry any Frenchman with a memory of the last thirty years, but a fact to be faced.

In other respects France was moving closer to compatible relationships with Germany, and with her other European neighbors. It was increasingly apparent that France's prosperity as well as her security was inexorably bound to the western European community at large. Old feuds were less important than new needs. French initiative was in good part responsible for the formation in 1952 of a European Coal and Steel Community, in which she agreed with West Germany and the three Benelux countries to pool certain resources, regulate prices, and jointly control production for the benefit of the group at large. In January, 1958, another development, known as the European Economic Community but soon to be called the Common Market, proposed to bring those countries into a broader association that would eventually open a wide area with millions of people to free trade and a common labor pool with equally controlled wages. The problems raised by that farsighted joint plan have not yet been resolved.

German troops parading through the place de la Concorde, June, 1940

The most agonizing problem France had to face in the 1950s involved the disintegration of her colonial empire, a problem which, before it was solved, destroyed the Fourth Republic and brought the nation almost to the point of another bloody revolution. Immediately after the World War the Vietnamese in Indochina under Ho Chi-Minh, who won the recognition of Communist China and the Soviet Union, asserted their independence. It was the start of a long and costly conflict that to all intents finally ended (in spite of technical aid and financial assistance from the United States) with the defeat of the French forces at Dien Bien Phu in 1954. Peace was negotiated at Geneva, resulting in a division of Vietnam roughly along the Seventeenth Parallel. About ninety-two thousand French soldiers had died during those years and many more were wounded, including a large number of officers; France's pride had suffered; the French treasury was strained; France had lost its richest colony; and nothing lasting had been accomplished—grim realities of the sort the United States was also to face in the long, trying years to come.

One after another French colonies demanded independence, and gained it—many in a spirit of friendliness, others only after bitter and bloody proceedings. In 1956 both Tunisia and Morocco, stirred by a wave of Arab nationalism to dissatisfaction with their status as protectorates, won full independence without serious difficulty. Algeria was a different matter. An active war of rebellion broke out there just six months after Dien Bien Phu and lasted for eight long years, costing billions of dollars, hundreds of thousands of lives, and an almost complete demoralization of French spirit.

From the beginning of hostilities France had to contend with two opponents: the rebellious Algerian natives and the European settlers, more than a million of them, many with deep roots, who were determined to suppress the Arab natives and keep Algeria French. There were also more than a half million French troops in Algeria, some of whose commanding officers assumed an independent, aggressive policy toward the rebels that was directly contrary to the conciliation proposed from Paris and that, it seemed, could not be controlled from Paris. Savage reprisals on both sides were reported from the torn country. Bombings, torture, and the murder of civilians were reportedly routine. In May, 1958, while the government in Paris floundered, a

Charles de Gaulle's triumphant re-entry into Paris, August 26, 1944

combination of military and civilian activists in Algeria set up a Committee of Public Safety that threatened to become a rival government. Revolt was imminent, one that could easily cross over into France itself and detonate the explosive forces that had been charged by the Algerian controversy. Paratroopers from Algeria were actually dropped in Corsica where they were enthusiastically welcomed by supporters of the Algiers movement. Rumors were rife that they would soon drop in France.

This crisis ended the Fourth Republic. France was frightened enough; and the army was eager enough, to call De Gaulle back to power, virtually on his own terms, as the only Frenchman who could rally his countrymen to a common cause and avert the threatening disaster. He immediately went to Algeria where, without making any concessions, he averted civil war by his assumed authority and his prestige. That much accomplished, he called for a completely revised constitution which, when it was proposed by referendum in September, 1958, was overwhelmingly approved. Among other provisions this new document gave unprecedented authority to the office of the president. France had entered the "De Gaulle era."

The Algerian question was far from settled. While De Gaulle moved with caution the military became restive. When, in January, 1961, it was agreed by another referendum that Algerian voters should be able to choose among complete independence, autonomy, or integration with France, the commanding officers of the army in Algeria almost immediately attempted a military coup to forestall any possibility of native Algerian control of the local government. Such was their success at the start that once again France prepared for an invasion of paratroopers from Africa, and tanks and troops were assembled in the courtyards of the Louvre to repel them; people in and about Paris were urged to proceed to local airfields and reason with the invaders when they appeared. However, the revolt misfired. Although terrorism on both sides continued, both in Algeria and France, and attempts were made to assassinate De Gaulle, in July, 1962, Algeria voted for independence. Eight years of sanguinary conflict had ended; 750,000 of the Europeans, including members of families that had been there for a century or more, elected to leave North Africa for new lives elsewhere.

Half a million troops could now be brought back to France and

A steel mill in Louvain, France

De Gaulle could point out that, with her overseas empire virtually liquidated, for the first time since the Second World War France had no military operations to maintain anywhere. With her forces reorganized and equipped with her own atomic weapons, France could now look to her own security in a still troubled world. With this measure of assurance, De Gaulle gradually reduced France's role in NATO until, in March, 1966, he removed French troops from the NATO command and NATO headquarters and all American military installations from French soil.

For the eleven years of his tenure De Gaulle dominated the French scene as few if any leaders ever had in the history of all previous republics. During that period there were but three premiers, in dramatic contrast to the very rapid turnover in that office in preceding years. In 1963, by means that many qualified critics considered illegal, he persuaded his countrymen to agree to a constitutional amendment whereby the president would, at last, be elected by direct vote of the people instead of by an electoral college, as had been the case since the beginning of the Third Republic. He wanted to be not only head of state but leader of France (a title the opposition equated with *Führer*), standing above any reliance on parlement. Then and in years to come that isolation of the presidency from direct parliamentary control gave cause for serious disquiet. If the people did not give him his way, he had said he would resign (implying that France would then return to chaos), and he probably would have done so. In 1965, at the age of 75, he was elected to a second seven-year term, but only after a runoff election. The crisis came in 1969, following a year of violent student uprisings and a great wave of sympathetic strikes that nearly paralyzed the nation and almost destroyed the Fifth Republic. De Gaulle again proposed constitutional reforms, submitting them to a national plebiscite and again threatening to resign if he were rebuffed. This time he failed to win a majority (he obtained only 47 per cent of the votes) and he did in fact resign within a day. The election of Georges Pompidou caused no serious tremors within the nation.

When De Gaulle died in 1970 his concept of the "grandeur of France" died with him. His impact on his times cannot yet be fairly appraised. However, it is possible to recall some of the developments in France that coincided with the years of his administration. It was during the 1960s that the traditional artisan economy of the nation rapidly gave way to technological progress that converted France into one of Europe's leading industrial powers. French industry actually grew at a higher rate than even that of West Germany or the United States. From the 1940s through the 1960s the population increased because of a rising birth rate (referred to as "le bébé-boom") and steady immigration, which put growing demands on the industrial machine and at the same time provided the manpower to service it. This belated industrial revolution is far from complete, but it has already left its mark almost everywhere, not only in the big new factories joining the ruined castles and abbeys along the Seine valley and elsewhere, the tractors in the fields, and the great hydroelectric installations rising along the Loire River and in the Auvergne, but in the pages of popular magazines where advertisements once concentrating on food, drink, and underwear, devote themselves increasingly to the latest luxury gadgets, such as electric refrigerators, dishwashers, and camping equipment. (The use of English and American words and phrases add snob appeal to the attraction of the products.) Automobile registration has soared. Between 1957 and 1965 the number of television sets increased more than tenfold; and so on.

De Gaulle appointed André Malraux minister of cultural affairs, and under his direction the time-blackened monuments of Paris were scoured of their sooty film; certain neglected historical districts of the city, such as the Marais, were restored to a semblance of their former elegance. At Versailles, along the Loire valley, and elsewhere in the country *son et lumière* festivals celebrated the ancient glories of France.

More painfully than in most countries, France is torn between the lure of its past and the tug of its future. The choice of values is not easy. Paris and other French cities are now ringed about by seemingly interminable megalithic blocks of apartments and industrial plants. But the nation is still relatively underpopulated. One does not have to go far into the countryside to discover *la douce France* of other days, and to understand the traditional German phrase, "Happy as God in France," recalling the envy with which her neighbors long viewed this favored land. France still remains, as Strabo remarked two thousand years ago, a land "designed by nature to accommodate the various needs and wants of man."

CHRONOLOGY

c. 15,000–10,000 B.C.	Peak period of Paleolithic art; paintings at Lascaux
600	Greeks colonize Massilia (Marseilles) in Gaul
500	Celts invade Gaul from across the Rhine
58–51	Julius Caesar conquers Gaul
52	Vercingetorix' native revolt is quelled by Caesar
A.D. 250	Martyrdom of Saint Denis (patron saint of France)
257	Franks and Alamanni invade Gaul from across the Rhine
451	A Gallo-Roman army defeats the Huns under Attila
481–511	Reign of Clovis (*first of the Merovingian rulers*)
732	Charles Martel's victory over the Moors at Tours
747–768	Reign of Pepin the Short (*first of the Carolingian rulers*)
771–814	Reign of Charlemagne
987–996	Reign of Hugh Capet (*first of the Capetian rulers*)
1066	William, duke of Normandy, conquers England
1095	Pope Urban II launches Crusades at Clermont-Ferrand
1100–1300	The rise of towns; construction of great cathedrals; flourishing of medieval art and literature
1180–1223	Reign of Philip II (Augustus), the "maker of Paris"
1226–1270	Reign of Louis IX (Saint Louis)
1285–1314	Reign of Philip IV (the Fair)
1305	Election of Clement V, a Frenchman, as pope
1309–1377	The Avignon papacy
1328–1350	Reign of Philip VI (*first of the Valois rulers*)
1337–1453	The Hundred Years' War with England
1378–1417	The Great Schism in the Church
1428–1429	Joan of Arc enables Charles VII to be crowned at Reims
1449–1461	Expulsion of the English from France
1515–1547	Reign of Francis I
1562–1598	Civil and religious wars of the Reformation
1589–1610	Reign of Henry IV (*first of the Bourbon rulers*)
1598	The Edict of Nantes grants religious equality to Huguenots
1610–1643	Reign of Louis XIII
1624–1642	Cardinal Richelieu administers France
1631–1648	France fights in the Thirty Years' War
1643–1715	Reign of Louis XIV (the Sun King)
1648–1653	The *Fronde* uprisings
1685	Revocation of the Edict of Nantes; Huguenots exiled
1701–1714	French hegemony is reduced in War of the Spanish Succession
1715–1774	Reign of Louis XV; the monarchy declines in importance

1720	John Law's "Mississippi Bubble" bursts
1741	France enters the War of the Austrian Succession
c. 1750	The French Enlightenment
1756–1763	The Seven Years' War (the French and Indian Wars); France loses most of her overseas possessions
1774–1792	Reign of Louis XVI, France's last absolute monarch
1778–1783	France intervenes in the War of American Independence
1789	The French Revolution begins
1792	Abolition of the monarchy; a republic is declared
1792–1793	A coalition of European powers unite against France
1793–1794	The Reign of Terror
1795	Adoption of the Metric System
1799–1804	The Consulate establishes the dictatorship of Napoleon
1804	Napoleon crowns himself emperor of France; his *Civil Code* becomes law
1812	Napoleon's armies are driven from Russia
1814	Napoleon is exiled to Elba; restoration of Louis XVIII
1815	Napoleon returns, is defeated, and is banished
1830	The July Revolution; Charles X is deposed; accession of Louis Philippe II (of the house of Orleans)
1848	Louis Philippe abdicates; the Second Republic begins
1852–1870	The Second Empire under Napoleon III
1854	France and Russia battle in the Crimean War
1870	War with Prussia; Napoleon III abdicates; the Third Republic is proclaimed
1871	France is defeated by Prussia, relinquishing Alsace and Lorraine; the Communard Riots
1894–1906	The Dreyfus Affair
1914–1918	World War I
1919	The Versailles Treaty; Alsace and Lorraine are returned
1936	A Socialist coalition government under Léon Blum
1939	World War II begins
1940	France falls to the Germans; General Charles de Gaulle organizes the French resistance
1940–1944	The Vichy Regime under Petain and Laval
1944	Allied forces free France from German occupation
1944–1946	De Gaulle heads a provisional government
1946–1958	The Fourth Republic
1954	France loses Indochina
1958	The Fifth Republic is established
1958–1969	The presidency of Charles de Gaulle
1962	Algeria wins independence after an eight-year struggle
1968	Student uprisings; workmen's strikes
1969	De Gaulle loses a plebiscite and resigns; Georges Pompidou is elected president

CREDITS AND INDEX